SOUTHERN on a SHOESTRING

"**Southern on a Shoestring** is full of easy yet elegant recipes for every occasion. I know that this book is going to be used at my parties for a very long time!"

— **Dorothy Kern**
Creator of popular blog *Crazy for Crust*
and author of *Dessert Mash-Ups*

"From modern offerings such as Turtle Cheese Ball and Veggie Pasta Skillet to the more traditional chicken and dumplings and pecan pie, **Southern Cooking on a Shoestring** provides over 70 delicious, step-by-step recipes. I love that none of McCallie's dishes require hours spent standing at the stove or shopping for costly, hard-to-find ingredients. All can be made easily and inexpensively. This is a delightful cookbook for cost-conscious, time-pressed cooks. It's also a smart and effortless way to add a taste of the South to my kitchen."

— **Kathy Hunt**
Author of *Fish Market and Herring: A Global History*, food writer for
Zester Daily and *Reuters Media Express*, and a freelance journalist

"**Southern on a Shoestring** is the quintessential Southern cookbook. Kim McCallie's recipes are a delicious mix of tried-and-true classics along with fresh takes on old favorites, and she provides excellent advice on how to stock a well-rounded pantry so you can make these recipes without breaking the bank. Beautifully written and photographed, the stories enthrall and the photographs entice! If you love Southern food, this book should be a part of your collection!"

— **Kelly Jaggers**
Author of *The Everything Easy Asian Cookbook*
and of food blog evilshenanigans.com

"A profound love of food and family emerges as you read through the pages of Kim McCallie's first book. And anyone in charge of feeding a family will appreciate recipes that won't break your budget or find you spending all day in the kitchen to prepare them."

— **Faye Porter**
Author of *At My Grandmother's Table*
and *At My Grandmother's Knee*

"A must-have for every home! Kim perfectly brings together delicious and traditional Southern food with contemporary preparation methods for the busy cook on a budget. The Sausage and Potato Bake is a new staple for my family."

— **Ashton Swank**
Author of *Party Popcorn*
and of blog *Something Swanky*

SOUTHERN on a SHOESTRING

Kimberly McCallie

FRONT TABLE BOOKS
AN IMPRINT OF CEDAR FORT, INC.
SPRINGVILLE, UTAH

ISBN 13: 978-1-4621-1851-9

Published by Front Table Books, an imprint of Cedar Fort, Inc.
2373 W. 700 S., Springville, UT 84663
Distributed by Cedar Fort, Inc., www.cedarfort.com

LIBRARY OF CONGRESS CATALOGING-IN-PUBLICATION DATA
Names: McCallie, Kimberly, 1969- author.
Title: Southern on a shoestring / Kimberly McCallie.
Description: Springville, Utah : Front Table Books, an imprint of Cedar Fort,
   Inc., [2016] | Includes index.
Identifiers: LCCN 2016003789 (print) | LCCN 2016014395 (ebook) | ISBN
   9781462118519 (perfect bound : acid-free paper) | ISBN 9781462126453
   (epub, pdf, mobi)
Subjects: LCSH: Cooking, American--Southern style. | Cooking--Southern
   states. | LCGFT: Cookbooks.
Classification: LCC TX715.S68 M33 2016 (print) | LCC TX715.S68 (ebook) | DDC
   641.5975--dc23
LC record available at http://lccn.loc.gov/2016003789

Cover and page design by M. Shaun McMurdie
Cover design © 2016 Cedar Fort, Inc.
Edited by Melissa J. Caldwell

Printed in the United States of America

10 9 8 7 6 5 4 3 2 1

Printed on acid-free paper

To my husband, Eric,
who believed in me from the moment we met

CONTENTS

Desserts

ACKNOWLEDGMENTS

I would like to thank everyone who has played a role in my life throughout the years. Some of you have inspired me. A few of you have amused me. But all of you have encouraged me, and I am forever grateful.

To my sons, Baylor and Cullen McCallie, who have challenged me from the beginning and will inspire me until the end. I do it all for you.

To my parents, Duke and Susan Fort, who showed me how to live and are always there for me.

To my dearest friends Christine Hansen and Julia Jerome, who started this food festival madness with me years ago. No time has passed when we're together. I admire the strong women you have become.

To Deborah Smith, who shared office space, recipes, and wild tales with me. You endured hearing about my dream more than anyone, and you were the first person to believe in me. You're one of my favorite people.

To Greg Arnsdorff, who taught me that loving yourself is the greatest love of all. More important, you taught me the difference between a true leader and someone in a leadership role. I'm grateful that you allowed your spotlight to briefly illuminate my little corner of the world.

To my closest friend, confidant, and mentor, Judith Shuman. When you told me that I could do this, I believed you. This would not have happened without you. Thank you for seeing more in me than I could see in myself.

WHERE MY STORY BEGINS

Sometimes, inspiration comes when you least expect it, and you didn't even know you needed to be inspired. In the summer of 2009, my son asked me what I dreamed of becoming when I grew up. I told him that I had dreamed of being a writer. His eight years on this earth had turned him into quite the pessimist: "A writer? Who would read it?"

A couple of weeks later, he brought up the subject again. "What was that dream you had, the one that never came true?" And for the first time, I wondered how I would ever be able to encourage my children to follow their dreams if I didn't at least attempt to follow my own.

So what would I write about and how would I begin? I chose to write about my favorite subject—food—and hoped that it would interest other people as well. Even though many of us are struggling to make ends meet in the current economy, we still find pleasure in food, from a simple dinner of rice and beans to the occasional splurge of filet mignon. Food nourishes, comforts, and unifies. Sharing recipes and discussing food breaks down all social barriers.

In August 2010, I began writing my food blog, *A Well-Seasoned Life*, as a way to open my kitchen to readers by sharing my recipes, cookbook reviews, restaurant reviews, and personal essays. Most of my recipe posts include helpful tips and step-by-step instructions to ensure success in the kitchen. I also don't believe it should cost a fortune to prepare a delicious meal, so most of my recipes are prepared with seasonal and affordable ingredients.

INTRODUCTION

The only images that some people have of life in the South are the beautifully and richly stylized photographs seen in Southern lifestyle magazines and cookbooks. As a Southerner, I too have been drawn in by the fantasy presented on those pages. But that is exactly what that lifestyle is—a fantasy. The reality is that the majority of people, no matter where they're from, are working with limited budgets and are simply trying to put a delicious yet affordable meal on the table for their families. With this cookbook, I hope to show readers that the spirit of Southern cooking can be captured regardless of location and without financial sacrifice. For me, the spirit of Southern cooking is defined in two ways: by the ingredients, and by the attitude in which the ingredients are used.

Throughout my marriage, I have been both a stay-at-home mom and a full-time working-outside-of-the-home mom. No matter which role I've played, I have always been conscious of the cost of food and the amount of money that I spend on feeding my family. One of the main ways that I cut the cost of cooking is by keeping a full pantry of essential ingredients. These essential ingredients are different for everyone, based on the recipes that your family prefers. As you read through this cookbook, you will see that I use some of the same ingredients in many recipes. Those are the ingredients that I keep in abundance in my pantry. And because there is an abundance of those ingredients, I create as many recipes with those ingredients as I can.

My first approach, and one that I would encourage everyone to try, when reading a cookbook or trying a new recipe is to choose recipes that call for ingredients already in my pantry. Experimenting with new ingredients can be expensive if those ingredients aren't part of your normal shopping trip. However, there is always a sense of excitement when I splurge on new bottles of spices or sauces. These small indulgences can easily renew my interest in cooking and experimenting in the kitchen.

My goal with this cookbook is to create recipes that use affordable ingredients and are easy to create. Many of these recipes have been requested of me time and time again. May they become part of your repertoire as well.

APPETIZERS

Becoming the Reluctant Entertainer

A rite of passage for many females is the first time we're allowed to attend a bridal or baby shower with our mothers. I remember being wedged on a couch between my mother and a cousin, anxiously waiting to see what would happen next or, more important, what food would be served. Small bowls of peanuts and pastel butter cream mints were placed strategically around the room to keep the wolves at bay until the food was ready to serve. I gravitated toward the mints, while my cousin stuck close to the peanuts. Every time I see a bag of those mints hanging in the candy aisle, it takes me back to my childhood and those afternoons spent with family and friends.

While my husband is able to remember when and where he was the first time he heard a song, I can remember the exact moment that I was introduced to certain foods for the first time. During one particular shower, my cousin and I were circling the refreshments when our eyes were drawn to a large orange ball covered in chopped pecans in the middle of the table. Yes, it was the first time either of us had ever seen a cheese ball. When I inquired about its identity and was told it was a cheese ball, I decided to pass. Cheese is not my friend. My cousin, being a cheese fanatic, helped herself to a generous portion and regretted that move soon after. "I took too much. It's really dense."

Years later, I was a bridesmaid in one of my high school friend's weddings and attended a shower hosted by her future sister-in-law, in her honor. At that shower, I was introduced to my friend's relatives and the cucumber sandwich. The cucumber sandwich and I have remained close.

In these memories, food plays the main role. Unfortunately, I can't always remember the guest of honor or the reason for the shower, but I can always tell you what food was served and if I enjoyed it.

While I do not consider myself an entertainer or a natural-born hostess, I do understand the importance of offering delicious appetizers and finger foods at a gathering. The food, good or bad, is what will be remembered at the end of the event.

The recipes that I've included here have been eaten and requested many times over the years. Guests will remember when they ate these dishes and who prepared them.

BLACK-EYED PEAS
& Ham Dip

Many years ago, my coworkers and I decided that we needed more reasons to celebrate with food. We started hosting "festivals" on a regular basis in which we would bring various finger foods to the office and graze all day long. My friend Julia brought in this dip, and it's one of my favorites. Warm and savory, it is one comforting appetizer.

8 oz. diced cooked ham

1 medium onion, finely diced

½ green bell pepper, finely diced

1 Tbsp. olive oil

1 jalapeño, deseeded and finely diced

2 (15-oz.) cans of seasoned southern-style black-eyed peas, undrained

1 cup mild shredded cheddar cheese

1 tsp. garlic salt

1 tsp. black pepper

2 Tbsp. hot sauce

2 pkgs. corn chip scoops

1. In a skillet over medium heat, sauté ham, onion, and bell pepper with olive oil until vegetables are soft and caramelized, 8–10 minutes.

2. Pour the ham and vegetable mixture into a slow cooker. Add the remaining ingredients except the corn chips.

3. Stir to blend and cook on low until warmed through, at least two hours. Flavors improve the longer the dip cooks.

4. Serve with corn chip scoops.

HOT BUFFALO CHICKEN
& Bacon Dip

I often try to re-create restaurant food at home. One of my favorite dips is from a famous chicken wing restaurant chain and features warm chicken, ranch dressing, and bacon. This recipe pays homage to that dish and saves money by keeping the family at home.

1 tsp. olive oil

2 boneless chicken breasts, cubed into small pieces

4 Tbsp. butter or margarine

½ cup hot sauce

2 (8-oz.) pkgs. cream cheese, softened

1 (1-oz.) pkg. ranch dressing mix

½ pkg. real bacon bits

5–6 green onions, thinly sliced (set aside one onion for garnish)

1 cup shredded cheddar cheese

your favorite corn chip scoops for serving

1. Preheat oven to 350 degrees.
2. In a small skillet, heat olive oil and add chicken. When chicken is golden brown and cooked through, add butter and hot sauce.
3. Cook for an additional 2–3 minutes until chicken is well coated. Remove from heat.
4. In a small mixing bowl, add cream cheese and ranch dressing mix and stir until well blended.
5. In a small baking dish, spread cream cheese and ranch mixture.
6. Sprinkle bacon bits and most of the green onions on top of the cream cheese mixture.
7. Add the seasoned chicken on top of the bacon and onions.
8. Bake in the oven for approximately 20 minutes, or until heated through.
9. Add cheddar cheese on top of chicken and put back in oven until cheese has melted.
10. Remove from oven and sprinkle on remaining green onions.
11. Serve warm with scoop chips or crackers.

HONEY MUSTARD
Kielbasa Bites

The kielbasa is my favorite sausage. Whenever I find them on sale, I stock up and put several in my freezer. They thaw quickly in the refrigerator or microwave and provide me with a quick appetizer or dinner. This appetizer combines some of my favorite ingredients— kielbasa, bacon, and mustard—into satisfying little bites perfect for parties, tailgating, or just plain snacking.

1 (16-oz.) pkg. bacon, cut in half

14 oz. kielbasa sausage

SAUCE:

½ cup yellow mustard

¼ cup honey

¼ tsp. black pepper

1 Tbsp. Worcestershire sauce

1 tsp. balsamic vinegar

1. Preheat oven to 350 degrees.
2. To prepare sausage, first cut bacon in half and count the number of slices. Next, cut sausage into the same number of pieces as bacon. Wrap a piece of bacon around a sausage and secure with a toothpick.
3. Line a large baking dish with foil and grease with cooking spray. Add wrapped sausages to dish and bake for 30 minutes.
4. While the sausages are baking, prepare the sauce. Put all ingredients in a small bowl and blend until smooth.
5. After sausages have cooked for 30 minutes, take them out of the oven. Drain off any excess oil.
6. Pour sauce evenly over the sausage bites and return to oven for an additional 20 minutes. Keep an eye on sausages so they don't overcook.
7. Immediately remove sausages from baking dish and put on a serving dish.

HOT
Onion Dip

At one point in my food-writing career, I penned a weekly food column for my local newspaper. I would occasionally have recipes given to me to consider for an article. This recipe came to me from two ladies from my area, Diane and Harriett, and it is wonderful. It's hard to believe that onions and cheese can come together to make such a special dish.

3 (8-oz.) pkgs. cream cheese, softened

½ cup mayonnaise

1½ cups freshly grated Parmesan cheese

4 cups chopped onions

OPTIONAL:

for additional flavor, add either black pepper, cayenne pepper, hot sauce, Worcestershire sauce, or garlic sauce to taste.

your favorite corn scoop chips

1. Preheat oven to 400 degrees.

2. In a large bowl, mix together cream cheese, mayonnaise, and cheese. If you're using one of the optional spices, add that now. After cheese mixture is smooth, stir in the onions.

3. Pour into a greased 2-quart baking dish and bake for 20 minutes until brown and bubbly.

4. Serve with your favorite scoop chips.

ROASTED
Shrimp Cocktail

Roasting shrimp is a quick and easy way to prepare a shrimp cocktail. Tossed with garlic and olive oil, these shrimp can be seasoned to suit your taste.

½ lb. large shrimp

2 cloves garlic, finely chopped

1 Tbsp. olive oil

sprinkle of salt and seafood seasoning

OPTIONAL:

cocktail sauce or tartar sauce

1. Heat oven to 450 degrees.
2. Put foil on a large baking pan and grease with cooking spray. Set aside.
3. In a medium bowl, add shrimp, garlic, olive oil, and seasoning. Toss until well coated and place on prepared baking pan.
4. Roast five minutes. Toss with a spoon.
5. Roast for an additional five minutes until done.
6. Serve with your favorite sauce.

Creamy Ranch
PINWHEELS

This is the pinwheel that started it all and became a jumping-off point for all other pinwheels to follow. These are excellent by themselves but serve as a good base for any other ingredients that you may want to add. My friend Julia introduced these to our food festivals and served them with some salsa spooned on top.

3 (8-oz.) pkgs. cream cheese, softened

2 (1-oz.) pkgs. ranch dressing mix

3 green onions, thinly sliced

8 flour tortillas, burrito size

1. In a medium mixing bowl, blend cream cheese, ranch dressing mix, and green onions until smooth.

2. Spread ⅛ of mixture evenly over a flour tortilla, leaving a small border around edge. Roll tortillas as tightly as possible and wrap in a piece of plastic wrap. Secure the sides of the plastic wrap. Repeat with each tortilla.

3. Refrigerate rolls until chilled, preferably overnight.

4. Before serving, cut off ends and save for snacking. Slice roll into even pieces, approximately eight slices per roll.

Turkey Club PINWHEELS

Ah, the pinwheel . . . that divine combination of cream cheese filling and flour tortilla. I love thee so. I'm always drawn to a platter of pinwheels whether they're homemade or store bought. They're so satisfying. These turkey club pinwheels loaded with turkey and bacon will satisfy any pinwheel lover.

SPREAD

1 (8-oz.) pkg. cream cheese, softened

½ tsp. black pepper

1 tsp. garlic powder

1 Tbsp. paprika

1 Tbsp. hot sauce

½ tsp. garlic salt

PINWHEELS

8 flour tortillas, burrito size

16 pieces thinly sliced deli-style turkey

16 strips prepared bacon

1 cup fresh spinach

1 cup shredded cheddar cheese

1. Put all of the ingredients for the spread in a small bowl and, using a mixer, combine until smooth.

2. To make a pinwheel, spread about ⅛ of the spread mixture evenly on one flour tortilla. Leave a small border around the edge of the tortilla.

3. Add two slices of turkey side-by-side on top of spread. Tear or dice two slices of bacon into small pieces and sprinkle over turkey. Lay several pieces of spinach horizontally right down the center of tortilla. Sprinkle whole tortilla with cheddar cheese.

4. Roll tortilla as tightly as possible and immediately wrap in a piece of plastic wrap. Secure the sides of the plastic wrap. Repeat with each tortilla.

5. Refrigerate rolls until chilled, preferably overnight.

6. Before serving, cut off ends and save for snacking. Slice roll into even pieces, approximately 8 slices per roll.

Pepperoni Pizza
PINWHEELS

Perfect the way they are, these pinwheels only get better dipped into warm marinara sauce.

3 (8-oz.) pkgs. cream cheese, softened

½ tsp. garlic salt

½ tsp. Italian seasoning

8 flour tortillas, burrito size

¾ cup marinara sauce

1 cup pepperoni, cut into quarters

1 cup shredded mozzarella cheese

1. In a medium mixing bowl, blend cream cheese, garlic salt, and Italian seasoning until smooth. Spread ⅛ of mixture evenly over a flour tortilla, leaving a small border around the edge.

2. Spread approximately 2 tablespoons of marinara sauce evenly over cream cheese mixture. Place ⅛ of pepperoni pieces over marinara sauce and sprinkle with mozzarella cheese.

3. Roll tortillas as tightly as possible and wrap in a piece of plastic wrap. Secure the sides of the plastic wrap. Repeat with each tortilla.

4. Refrigerate rolls until chilled, preferably overnight. Before serving, cut off ends and save for snacking.

5. Slice roll into even pieces, approximately 8 slices per roll.

MEXICAN *Shrimp Cocktail* SPREAD

If you want to make a dish that everyone is going to go crazy over, then this is the recipe for you. I created this dish to celebrate Red Ribbon Week at work and it was a huge hit with many people asking me to share the recipe. I suggest spreading it out on a platter for optimum visual impact. It's a beauty!

3 (8-oz.) pkgs. cream cheese, softened

1 (1-oz.) pkg. ranch dressing mix

¾ cup salsa

2 (4-oz.) cans tiny shrimp, drained (or equivalent of regular shrimp, finely chopped)

sprinkle of garlic salt, to taste

3 green onions, thinly sliced

1 Tbsp. chopped cilantro

crackers, for serving

1. Using a mixer, blend together cream cheese and ranch dressing mix. Spread evenly into a serving dish.

2. Spoon salsa evenly over cream cheese mixture. Sprinkle shrimp over salsa. Lightly sprinkle shrimp with garlic salt. Sprinkle green onions and cilantro over shrimp.

3. Cover and refrigerate spread until thoroughly chilled.

4. Serve with crackers.

SAVORY
Chicken Spread

The first time I had this spread was at a family gathering and I couldn't stop eating it. My cousin Angela came up with this cream cheese–based spread as an alternative to traditional chicken salad with mayonnaise. This dish is one of our must-haves for any event.

3 (8-oz.) pkgs. cream cheese, softened

½ tsp. black pepper

2 (1-oz.) pkgs. ranch dressing mix

6 boneless chicken breasts, boiled and shredded

3 green onions, finely sliced

crackers, for serving

1. In a large bowl, cream together cream cheese, pepper, and ranch dressing mix until completely blended. Add shredded chicken and green onions. Stir until well blended.

2. The mixture will be thick and dense. Refrigerate until ready to serve.

3. Serve with crackers.

TIP: Serve with chicken-flavored crackers if you can find them.

BUFFALO
Chicken Spread

Using the savory chicken spread recipe as a base, I spiced it up by adding some hot sauce. If you prefer it even hotter, sprinkle in some cayenne pepper to taste.

3 (8-oz.) pkgs. cream cheese, softened

½ tsp. black pepper

2 (1-oz.) pkgs. ranch dressing mix

3 Tbsp. hot sauce

6 boneless chicken breasts, boiled and shredded

1 cup shredded cheddar cheese

3 green onions, thinly sliced

crackers, for serving

1. In a large bowl, cream together cream cheese, pepper, ranch dressing mix, and hot sauce until completely blended. Add shredded chicken, cheese, and green onions. Stir until well blended.

2. Refrigerate until ready to serve.

3. Serve with crackers.

LOADED *Chicken Salad* DEVILED EGGS

My husband and I are huge fans of both deviled eggs and chicken salad, so I thought, "Why not combine them?" These are unbelievably good and can really serve as a meal instead of an appetizer. These deviled eggs are the perfect way to serve leftover chicken salad.

6 eggs, boiled

½ lb. chicken, cooked and shredded

3 green onions, finely chopped

½ cup mayonnaise

1 tsp. yellow mustard

1 tsp. dijon mustard

⅛ tsp. black pepper

⅛ tsp. celery seed

⅛ tsp. garlic salt

⅛ tsp. paprika, plus additional paprika for garnish

1. Peel boiled eggs and cut them in half lengthwise. Remove egg yolks. Set egg whites aside.

2. In a small bowl, chop egg yolks and add remaining ingredients. Stir until well blended.

3. Carefully fill each egg white with chicken mixture.

4. Finish with a sprinkling of paprika, if desired.

CUCUMBER DILL
Cheese Ball

While I enjoy traditional cucumber sandwiches, I wanted to re-create the flavors of a cucumber sandwich into a cheese ball that could be prepared more quickly and transported more easily.

½ cup shredded cucumber

pinch of salt

1 (8-oz.) pkg. cream cheese, softened

1 tsp. lemon juice

1 tsp. garlic salt

1 tsp. finely chopped fresh dill

pita chips or pita bread, for serving

1. In a colander over a small bowl, add shredded cucumber and a pinch of salt. Allow the cucumber to drain to release excess water, 20–30 minutes.

2. Squeeze cucumber dry with a paper towel or tea towel.

3. In a small bowl, blend cream cheese, lemon juice, and garlic salt until smooth. Stir in drained cucumber and dill.

4. Refrigerate until ready to serve.

5. Serve with pita chips or pita bread.

TOFFEE
Apple Dip

This toffee apple dip recipe has been one of my most requested and enjoyed. I've prepared it for more events than I can count. I even know a few people to forgo the apples and graham crackers and eat it with a spoon. I suggest you prepare this the day before your event. As the toffee chips set overnight, they melt down and become gooey and delicious.

1 (8-oz.) pkg. cream cheese, softened

4 Tbsp. (½ stick) butter, softened

3 Tbsp. powdered sugar

½ cup brown sugar, firmly packed

1 tsp. vanilla

1 (8-oz.) pkg. toffee bits

sliced apples and graham cracker sticks, for serving

1. With the mixer on low, combine cream cheese and butter until well blended. Add powdered sugar, brown sugar, and vanilla. Mix until well blended.

2. Reserve about ¼ of the toffee chips and set aside.

3. Pour the rest of the toffee chips into the mixture and fold in with a spoon. Refrigerate the dip until well chilled, preferably overnight.

4. Right before serving, sprinkle the reserved toffee bits on top.

5. Serve with apples and graham cracker sticks.

TURTLE *Cheese Ball*

If you are a fan of turtle desserts—chocolate, caramel, and pecans—you'll need to include this cheese ball at your next event. It will definitely draw everyone's attention at the appetizer or dessert table. This recipe can go either way.

1 (8-oz.) pkg. cream cheese, softened

4 Tbsp. (½ stick) butter, softened

⅓ cup powdered sugar

½ cup packed brown sugar

1 tsp. vanilla

1 cup toffee chips

1 cup mini chocolate chips

chopped pecans for garnish, optional

graham crackers or apple slices, for serving

1. Cream together cream cheese and butter until smooth. Add powdered sugar, brown sugar, and vanilla. Blend until smooth.

2. Stir in the toffee chips and mini chocolate chips. Refrigerate for approximately a half hour.

3. After mixture has firmed up, lay some plastic wrap in a small bowl. Spoon mixture into bowl and use the wrap to form a ball. Refrigerate overnight.

4. Remove the plastic wrap, and flip cheese ball over onto your serving bowl or plate. This process will ensure the round shape you desire.

5. Press the chopped pecans into the cheese ball.

6. Serve with graham crackers or apple slices.

WHIPPED *Vanilla Dip*

My favorite way to serve this dip is on a platter surrounded by fresh strawberries and bite-size cubes of pound cake. It makes a beautiful presentation and is the perfect centerpiece for any event.

1 (8-oz.) pkg. cream cheese, softened

1 cup powdered sugar

1 tsp. vanilla

1 (8-oz.) whipped topping, thawed and divided

fresh fruit or cubed pound cake, for serving

1. With a mixer, blend cream cheese, powdered sugar, and vanilla until creamy.

2. Add half of whipped topping and blend in using mixer until well incorporated.

3. Fold in remaining whipped topping with a large spoon or rubber spatula.

4. Refrigerate until ready to serve.

5. Serve with fresh fruit or cubed pound cake.

WHIPPED *Chocolate Dip*

I often serve this chocolate dip alongside my whipped vanilla dip and toffee apple dip whenever I want to create a large display of fresh fruit, graham crackers, and cubed pound cake. You could also keep it simple—whipped chocolate dip and strawberries.

1 (8-oz.) pkg. cream cheese, softened

½ cup powdered sugar

2 Tbsp. cocoa powder

1 tsp. vanilla

1 (8-oz.) whipped topping, thawed and divided

fresh fruit or cubed pound cake, for serving

1. With a mixer, blend cream cheese, powdered sugar, cocoa, and vanilla together until creamy.

2. Add half of whipped topping and blend in using mixer until well incorporated.

3. Fold in remaining whipped topping with a large spoon or rubber spatula.

4. Refrigerate until ready to serve.

5. Serve with fresh fruit or cubed pound cake.

CINNAMON ROLL *Dippers*

Let's face it—the best part of cinnamon rolls is the cream cheese icing. Maybe I'm only speaking for myself. However, if you feel the same way, you'll want to try out this recipe so that you can satisfy your cream cheese icing craving.

DIPPERS

1 (7.5-oz.) can biscuits

¼ cup sugar

1 tsp. cinnamon

4 Tbsp. butter

CREAM CHEESE DIP

1 (8-oz.) pkg. cream cheese, softened

4 Tbsp. butter, softened

½ cup powdered sugar

1 tsp. vanilla

½ tsp. cinnamon

1. Preheat oven to 350 degrees.
2. For the dippers, prepare biscuits by cutting them into quarters.
3. In a small bowl, combine sugar and cinnamon. In another small bowl, melt butter in microwave. Dip each biscuit piece in melted butter and roll through the cinnamon-sugar mixture.
4. Place on a baking sheet lined with parchment paper.
5. Bake for approximately 10 minutes or until golden brown.
6. Serve dippers warm with cream cheese dip.
7. To make the dip, place all ingredients in a small bowl and mix until smooth.
8. Serve with dippers.

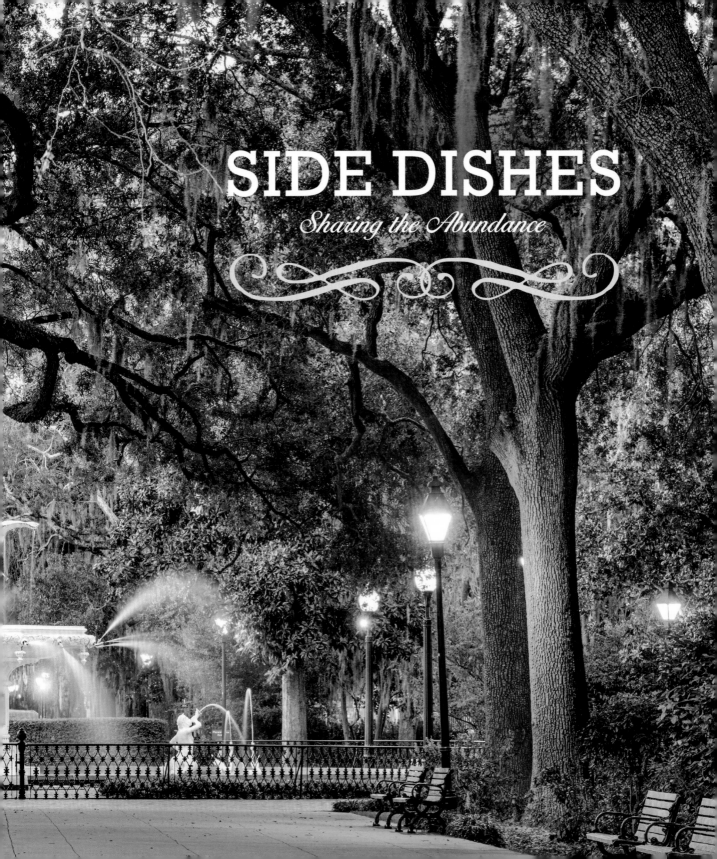

SIDE DISHES

Sharing the Abundance

As a child, I spent my summer days with my grandparents in the small town of Pineora, Georgia. Whenever I arrived at their house early in the mornings, I would find my grandparents already busy in the garden. Papa plowed row after row, the blades of his tiller throwing up the dark, rich dirt, the smell of it filling the air and creating a permanent memory of place and time. Mema, wearing a long-sleeved blouse to protect her arms from scratches, bugs, and sun exposure, dragged a five-gallon bucket with her down each row as she picked butter beans and field peas. And we grandchildren played among the plants, too young to help but old enough not to hinder.

In the afternoons, Mema would set to work in the kitchen preparing and preserving the harvest, removing corn from the cobs with a grater placed over a large bowl to catch all of the kernel's milky juices. She would set huge stockpots to simmering filled with gallons of creamed corn. Any hands that were available set to work shelling peas and beans. The only reward that we needed for our services at the end of the day was a chilled watermelon sliced in half and served on the front porch. ❧

Today, all across the country, gardens are bursting with an abundance of vegetables. Squash, zucchini, tomatoes, okra, broccoli, cauliflower, and cucumbers grow at such a rapid pace that you can barely keep up with them, picking the vegetables on a daily basis to avoid overgrowth and waste. There is a rush to preserve and to distribute the surplus.

Every gardener I've ever met has had a generous heart when it comes to sharing the harvest. Hating to see their hard work go to waste, they press bags full of vegetables into any open hands that they can find. And for those people who have no gardens of their own, the vegetables are welcome. I've seen the pleasure on people's faces whenever they've received a bag full of fresh vegetables. Isn't it satisfying to grow happiness in your own backyard?

I too know that feeling of gratitude because I've been fortunate enough to be on the receiving end of a gardener's generosity. I have welcomed bags of bell peppers, squash, and new potatoes from friends and family into my kitchen. While cooking these vegetables, it is nice to reflect upon the people who grew them and to enjoy the abundance of summer.

FOIL-WRAPPED
Potatoes & Onions

This is a dish that will always hold a special place in my heart because I will always associate it with Saturday night suppers with my husband and children. For almost 20 years now, we've been making this dish whenever we grill steaks, at least once a month. Every time that I open that foil and inhale the savory scent of onions and garlic, I think of how wonderful it smells. Just like home.

2 lb. potatoes (red potatoes, russets, or Yukon gold), peeled and sliced

1 onion, finely diced

6 cloves garlic, finely diced

2 Tbsp. olive oil

seasonings of your choice: I use a blend of seasoning salt, garlic salt, and black pepper

When preparing potatoes for this dish, you may choose to leave the peel on the potatoes, depending on your taste preference and the condition of the potato skin.

1. In a large bowl, add potatoes, onions, garlic, and olive oil. While I use a blend of my favorite seasonings above, you may choose to use your own seasoning favorites.

2. Prepare a large sheet of heavy-duty aluminum foil by greasing it with cooking spray.

3. Spread the potato mixture evenly over the foil. Fold up all four sides of the foil to create a packet.

4. Place the foil packet on the grill and cook on low heat for approximately 1 hour, checking carefully at the 30-minute mark. Potatoes should be tender and the onions and garlic should be caramelized.

5. Using an oven mitt, carefully remove the packet from the heat onto a plate. You may serve directly from the foil packet.

6. Serve with grilled steak, pork, or chicken.

ROASTED
Asparagus

Asparagus is one of those vegetables that I only buy when it's in season as it can be fairly expensive otherwise. It is my favorite green vegetable, and I eat it as much as I can when I find it for a good price. Asparagus doesn't need a lot of additional ingredients to make it delicious. A little olive oil and kosher salt will do the trick.

2 bunches of asparagus (approximately 2 lb.)

2 Tbsp. olive oil

¼ tsp. kosher salt

⅛ tsp. black pepper or lemon pepper

optional: zest of 1 lemon

1. Preheat oven to 400 degrees.

2. Line a baking sheet with aluminum foil and grease with cooking spray.

3. To prepare the asparagus, rinse under cold water and dry. Cut off tough ends. Lay asparagus in a single layer on the greased baking sheeting. Drizzle with olive oil and sprinkle with salt and pepper. Be sure to evenly distribute the oil and spices. Sprinkle on the lemon zest if you have some available.

4. Roast in the oven for approximately 20 minutes or until desired doneness. Some like firm asparagus, while others like it more tender, so cook times may vary based on preference.

5. Watch the dish carefully and use a spatula to move stalks around throughout the roasting process to keep them from sticking.

6. Serve immediately.

SAUTÉED SPINACH *with* Gaɾlic

I can never make enough of this recipe. No matter how many batches I make, hardly any of it makes it to the table for the actual meal as there is a lot of sampling done by my husband, my older son, and, of course, me. This is one of the quickest, easiest, and most delicious recipes in my cooking arsenal.

1 Tbsp. olive oil

2–3 cloves garlic, chopped

1 (6-oz.) bag fresh baby spinach

salt and black pepper, to taste

1. Heat olive oil in a large skillet over medium-high heat.
2. Add chopped garlic and cook for 1 minute, stirring continuously.
3. Add entire bag of spinach, lifting the oil and garlic from the bottom of the pan to top of spinach.
4. Season with salt and pepper. Cook for 2 minutes.
5. Serve immediately.

ROASTED
Brussels Sprouts

When a vegetable is cooked correctly and allowed to caramelize, it tastes better than candy. This is another one of those recipes that barely makes it to the table once I ask my husband if he wants a sample. He'll eat a few. I'll eat a few. And then . . . they're gone. When the bacon and soy sauce caramelize on the brussels sprouts, they create an addictive side dish.

1 bunch fresh brussels sprouts (approximately 1 lb.)

½ tsp. kosher salt

¼ tsp. black pepper

1 Tbsp. soy sauce

4 slices bacon, diced

1 Tbsp. olive oil

1. Preheat oven to 400 degrees.
2. Rinse brussels sprouts, cut off the stem, and slice each one in half. Place on a greased baking sheet.
3. Sprinkle evenly with salt and pepper. Drizzle with soy sauce.
4. Distribute bacon evenly over the brussels sprouts. Drizzle evenly with olive oil.
5. Roast in the oven for approximately 20 minutes until bacon is cooked and sprouts begin to caramelize around the edges, stirring often to prevent sticking.
6. Serve immediately.

ROASTED BROCCOLI WITH
Red Pepper Flakes

The recipe is equally as good prepared with cauliflower, or a combination of broccoli and cauliflower. Simply omit the red pepper flakes if you have mild taste buds.

1 lb. broccoli

1 Tbsp. olive oil

⅛ tsp. kosher salt

pinch of red pepper flakes

1. Preheat the oven to 400 degrees.

2. Cut the broccoli into bite-sized pieces. Place on a greased foil-lined baking pan. Drizzle with olive oil and sprinkle with kosher salt and red pepper flakes. (I use my hands to make sure that the olive oil and seasonings are equally distributed.)

3. Roast in the oven for about 15 minutes, stirring every few minutes to prevent burning. If you like your broccoli firm, remove after about 10 minutes; if you like your broccoli softer, cook a little longer.

4. Serve immediately.

Corn & Bacon SAUTÉ

My love of bacon is so strong that it makes me want to cry when I hear it sizzling in the skillet and smell the intoxicating aroma. The first bite into the salty smokiness completes me. Whenever I create a recipe, my first question to myself is, "How can I incorporate bacon into this dish?" Let's throw some onions, bacon, and corn together and see how it works out. It is a masterpiece.

½ medium onion, chopped

6 slices bacon, diced

1 tsp. olive oil

16 oz. frozen corn

seasonings: kosher salt, coarse black pepper, dried thyme

4–5 green onions, sliced

1. In a large skillet, sauté onion and bacon in olive oil on medium-low heat until bacon starts to get crisp, about 10 minutes.

2. After the bacon is crisp, remove bacon-onion mixture with a slotted spoon. Set aside.

3. Add the corn and seasonings to the skillet and cook on medium-high heat until the corn is heated through and moisture is cooked out.

4. Return the bacon-onion mixture back to the skillet and stir it all together.

5. Remove from heat.

6. Add green onions.

7. Serve immediately with your favorite pork or chicken dish.

FRIED CABBAGE
with
Bacon

When my husband and I started dating, he would cook for me quite often and introduced me to some dishes that I had never tried before. When he asked if I ate cabbage and bacon, I answered him with an emphatic yes! His fried cabbage and I became quick friends, thick as thieves. Later, on a visit to one of our favorite restaurants in Charleston, South Carolina, I asked the waitress about the vegetable of the day. She disappeared for a minute to inquire on the day's selection. She returned to the table with a sad scowl and informed in a disappointed tone that the answer was fried cabbage. I had a sharp intake of breath as I exclaimed, "I love fried cabbage!" I hope you will too.

1 whole cabbage

4–5 slices bacon

salt and black pepper, to taste

1. Cut cabbage into quarters and remove the core. Next, cut into bite-size pieces. Set aside.

2. Dice bacon and add to a large skillet, cooking bacon over medium heat until crisp. Remove bacon with a slotted spoon, reserving the bacon grease. Set bacon aside.

3. Add cabbage to bacon grease. Pepper can be added at this point; however, you should wait until the end of the cooking process to add salt to prevent the cabbage from become soggy.

4. Cook the cabbage on medium-high heat for 10–15 minutes, stirring frequently to bring the bacon grease from the bottom of the skillet and incorporating it throughout the cabbage. The edges of the cabbage should be golden brown.

5. Sprinkle in the desired amount of salt and add fried bacon back into the cabbage. Give it another quick stir to evenly distribute the salt and bacon.

6. Serve hot.

Squash Stuffing CASEROLE

This is one of those recipes that I pull out whenever I have an abundance of yellow squash, which happens quite often during the summers here in Georgia. I've often prepared it with a combination of squash and zucchini.

3 lb. yellow squash

1 large onion

¼ tsp. salt

¼ tsp. black pepper

½ cup water

2 (10.5-oz.) cans cream of chicken soup

1 (6-oz.) box of chicken-flavored stuffing mix

1. Preheat oven to 350 degrees.

2. In a large stockpot, combine yellow squash and onions with salt and pepper. Add a half cup of water and cook over medium heat for approximately 20 minutes until the vegetables are soft. Place the vegetables in a colander to drain.

3. In a large bowl, add the cream of chicken soup and stuffing mix. Add the drained squash and stir until combined.

4. Pour the mixture into a greased casserole dish and bake for 35–40 minutes until mixture is bubbly and golden brown.

5. This dish is perfect as a side for chicken and pork dishes.

SAVORY
Garden Casserole

I consider this a jazzed-up green bean casserole. If you throw in some diced chicken, you have a full meal in one dish.

2 (15-oz.) cans French-style green beans, drained

1 (15-oz.) can whole kernel corn, drained

2 (10.5-oz.) cans cream of mushroom soup

1 pkg. prepared boil-in-bag rice, or 1 cup of prepared rice

½ tsp. black pepper

½ tsp. garlic salt

1 (6-oz.) can fried onions, divided

1. Preheat oven to 350 degrees.
2. In a large mixing bowl, add all ingredients except fried onions. Add half of the fried onions to the bowl and set aside the remaining onions. Stir to combine and spread into a greased casserole dish.
3. Bake for approximately 40 minutes until heated through.
4. Sprinkle on remaining fried onions and bake for an additional five minutes.
5. Serve with your favorite chicken or pork dishes.

LOADED
Mashed Potato
CASSEROLE

Oh my! This casserole is divine. By adding the ham in addition to the bacon, this casserole could easily be a meal in itself instead of a side dish. I can guarantee that it will be one of the most delicious dishes on your table.

3 slices bacon, diced

8 oz. ham, diced

4 green onions, finely sliced and divided

2 lb. red potatoes, cubed

1 Tbsp. salt

½ cup or 1 stick butter or margarine, softened

½ cup sour cream

1½ cups shredded cheddar cheese, divided

¼ cup milk or buttermilk

¼ tsp. each black pepper, garlic salt, and seasoning salt

1. In a small skillet, fry bacon until crisp. Remove bacon with a slotted spoon. Set aside.

2. Add ham and three green onions to the bacon grease and cook until onions are softened.

3. In a large stockpot, add cubed potatoes and salt. Boil until potatoes are done, approximately 15 minutes.

4. When potatoes are done, drain and return to the stockpot. Add butter or margarine, sour cream, 1 cup of cheddar cheese, and milk. Using a potato masher, blend the ingredients together until desired consistency. Add seasonings to taste.

5. Stir in bacon, ham, and green onions. Pour into a greased casserole dish and sprinkle with remaining cheese and green onions.

6. Bake at 350 degrees until cheese is melted and ingredients are warmed through, 15–20 minutes.

7. This dish is perfect as a side with grilled meat.

RED RICE WITH
Sausage &
Tomatoes

Dear Red Rice,
I know that we have had a tumultuous relationship over the years. At times, I've hated you. You were overly dry and sickeningly sweet. At other times, you were perfectly cooked and seasoned, and I thought that we would always be friends. I keep getting pulled back into your drama every time I see you on a menu. But I hope that, with this recipe, we can settle our differences and live harmoniously.

Sincerely, Kim

In an attempt to adjust this traditional dish to suit my tastes, I have chosen to use diced tomatoes instead of tomato paste. The diced tomatoes add moisture and eliminate the concentrated sweetness of the paste.

6 pieces bacon, diced and divided

1 green bell pepper, finely diced

1 onion, finely diced

14 oz. kielbasa sausage, thinly sliced and quartered

2 cups red rice, uncooked

1 tsp. salt

½ tsp. chili powder

1 tsp. garlic powder

2 (15-oz.) cans diced tomatoes, with juice

4 cups chicken broth

1. Cook bacon until half done. Remove from grease and set aside.

2. Sauté peppers, onions, and sausage. Add rice and seasonings. Stir in tomatoes and chicken broth.

3. Pour in a greased casserole dish. Sprinkle with half of bacon.

4. Cover with foil and bake at 350 degrees for approximately 45 minutes. Test the doneness of the rice. It may need additional cook time based on the size of your dish.

5. Sprinkle with remaining bacon and return to oven until bacon is crispy.

6. Serve with your favorite seafood dish.

BAKED
Beefy Rice with
MUSHROOMS

For a number of years, I worked at a university, where I experienced some of the most stressful staff Christmas luncheons imaginable. By stressful, I mean that there were more people in attendance than there was food to serve. As someone who has prepared dishes for events, I am always concerned about the people-food ratio. More is better. Anyway, during these luncheons, I was able to wedge my way into line and get a small scoop of a dish that is similar to this one. I wanted to re-create the dish so that I could enjoy a full portion of the beefy, mushroom goodness.

1 medium onion, finely diced

1 Tbsp. olive oil

1 Tbsp. butter

8 oz. white mushrooms, sliced

½ tsp. black pepper

2 cups rice, uncooked

2 tsp. salt

1 Tbsp. reduced-sodium soy sauce

2 beef bouillon cubes

4 cups beef broth

1. Preheat oven to 350 degrees.
2. In a large skillet, sauté onions in olive oil for 3 minutes. Add butter and mushrooms. Sprinkle with pepper and sauté until mushrooms are soft, approximately 7 minutes.
3. Add rice, salt, soy sauce, and bouillon cubes. Stir until cubes are soft and can be smashed with the back of a spoon and evenly distribute into the rice mix.
4. Pour rice mix into a greased casserole dish.
5. Pour in beef broth.
6. Cover with foil and bake for approximately 45 minutes until broth is absorbed and rice is fluffy. Cook time may depend on the size of your casserole dish.
7. Serve with your favorite beef or pork dish.

HOMEMADE
Rice Pilaf

SIDE DISHES

Growing up, we always had a pot of rice on the table for dinner. Rice is a cheap way to stretch a meal. Plus, if you don't like something on your plate, you could easily fill up on rice. Rice is one of the ingredients that I always have in my pantry. Every now and then, I like to jazz it up by making my own box-style pilaf.

¼ cup vermicelli, broken into bite-size pieces

1 cup rice

1 tsp. olive oil

2½ cups chicken broth (or 2½ cups water plus 2 chicken bouillon cubes)

½ tsp. salt

½ tsp. dried parsley

1. In a medium saucepan, sauté the vermicelli and rice in olive oil until the vermicelli is golden brown.

2. Add the chicken broth (or water and bouillon combination), salt, and parsley. Bring to a boil.

3. Reduce heat to low and cook covered for 20 minutes, or until all liquid is absorbed.

4. This dish is perfect as a side for chicken or fish.

Veggie Pasta SKILLET

If I had my way, I would cook every meal in a skillet and would include different varieties of sautéed vegetables and pasta. But I also have a family that has to eat, so I don't always get my way. But when I do, I make a dish like this. Use whatever vegetables you like and have on hand.

2 Tbsp. olive oil

½ lb. asparagus (tough ends removed), cut into bite-size pieces

½ lb. yellow squash, thinly sliced

¼ red onion, thinly sliced

2 cloves garlic, finely diced

¼ tsp. black pepper

¼ tsp. garlic salt

8 oz. pasta, prepared

1. In a large skillet, heat olive oil over medium-high heat.

2. Add asparagus, squash, and onions, and sauté for 5 minutes.

3. Add garlic to the skillet and continue cooking vegetables until they reach your preferred tenderness.

4. Sprinkle in pepper and garlic salt.

5. Add in the cooked pasta and toss with vegetables until coated with olive oil and seasonings. If the dish seems dry, add more olive oil.

6. Adjust seasonings to taste.

7. Serve immediately.

MARINATED *Cucumber & Onion* SALAD

Quick and easy, this is the perfect side dish, especially if you have an abundance of cucumbers. I like my cucumbers crisp, so I always eat this salad a few hours after preparing. I then save the marinade and put fresh cucumbers in it the next day for some new crunch.

3–4 medium cucumbers (or one English cucumber), peeled (optional) and sliced

1 Vidalia onion (or red onion), thinly sliced

1 tsp. sugar

1 tsp. salt

½ tsp. black pepper

white vinegar

1. In a medium bowl, add cucumbers and onions. Sprinkle with seasonings.
2. Add enough vinegar to cover the cucumbers.
3. Cover and refrigerate until chilled.

Grape SALAD

While hosting a baby shower at work, one of my coworkers, Deborah, announced that she would be contributing a grape salad to the event. I was a little apprehensive to try it until she unveiled this gooey, creamy, brown sugar–laden delight. I put the leftovers in my office refrigerator and enjoyed them for the next couple of days.

1 (8-oz.) pkg. cream cheese, softened

1 (8-oz.) container sour cream

½ cup sugar

2 lb. seedless grapes (red, green, or combination)

2 Tbsp. margarine

¾ cup brown sugar

1½ cups chopped pecans

1. Mix together cream cheese, sour cream, and sugar.
2. Carefully stir in grapes. Set aside.
3. Melt margarine in the microwave and stir in brown sugar.
4. Spread the brown sugar mixture over the grapes.
5. Sprinkle the chopped nuts on top.
6. Refrigerate for several hours or overnight.
7. Just before serving, carefully stir mixture together.
8. Serve immediately.
9. Refrigerate any leftovers.

SIDE DISHES

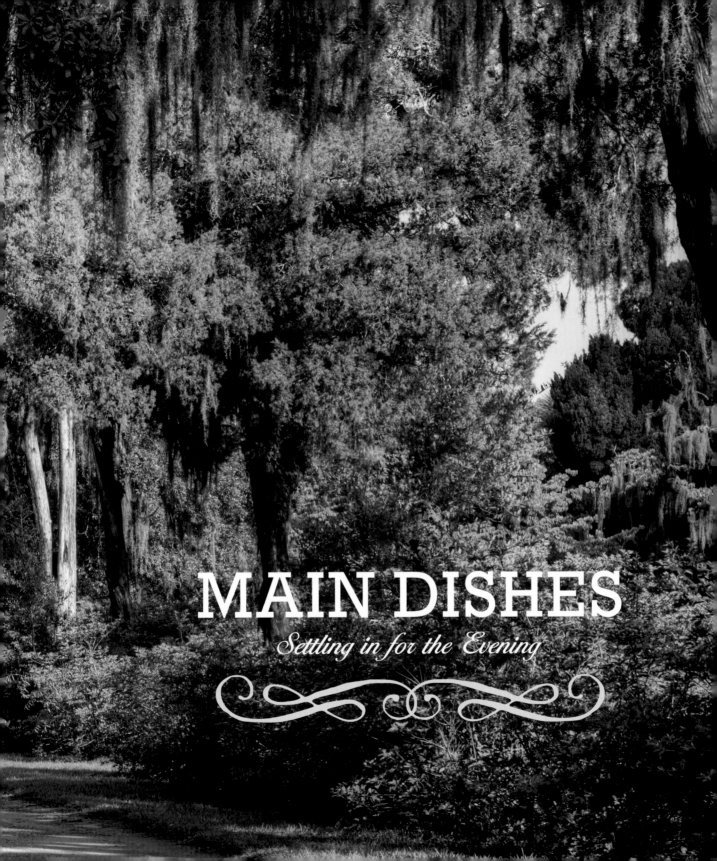

MAIN DISHES

Settling in for the Evening

I **know this confession** makes me sound so old, but I like to be at home before it gets dark. Not to say that I'm never out past dark, but I do prefer to be home by dusk, settling in for the evening. Just the phrase "settling in for the evening" is comforting to me.

If by some chance I am out at night driving home on lonely country roads, my eyes are drawn to the houses with their lights on and blinds open. I love to get that quick glimpse of a family sitting at the dining room table eating dinner and sharing their day.

While my family will occasionally go out to dinner on Friday nights, we always make sure that we're home on Saturday nights so that we can enjoy cooking and eating a meal together. About once or twice a month, 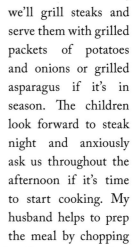 we'll grill steaks and serve them with grilled packets of potatoes and onions or grilled asparagus if it's in season. The children look forward to steak night and anxiously ask us throughout the afternoon if it's time to start cooking. My husband helps to prep the meal by chopping onions and garlic and peeling potatoes, while I season the steaks and prepare the packets for the grill. And every single time we do this, we marvel at how good life is.

MY FAMOUS
Chicken Salad

Of all the recipes in this cookbook, this is the main dish that I've made most often. It is also the recipe that is requested more than any other whenever I volunteer to cook for an event. I even got paid to make it one time. Sometimes people will tell me that they don't eat cilantro, so I just don't tell them that the salad contains cilantro. They eat it right up and go back for seconds.

1 chicken (or equivalent), roasted, skin removed, and shredded

½ bunch cilantro (approximately ½ cup), finely chopped

1 bunch green onions (approximately 6–8), thinly sliced

SPECIAL SAUCE

1 cup mayonnaise

2 Tbsp. dijon-style mustard

4–5 drops pepper sauce

¼ tsp. black pepper

¼ tsp. garlic salt

½ tsp. paprika

1. In a large bowl, add the shredded chicken, cilantro, and green onions. This is the perfect opportunity to incorporate a shortcut and use a rotisserie chicken from your local grocery store.

2. In a small bowl, mix all sauce ingredients together until smooth.

3. Taste the sauce before you add to the chicken to make sure the seasonings are to your taste.

4. Add to the chicken mixture and stir until fully incorporated.

5. Serve on buns or with your favorite crackers.

Chicken & DUMPLINGS

Chicken and dumplings are a labor of love, no matter how many shortcuts you take. This is a dish that I make on Sundays so that we can enjoy it all day long. A few years ago, I cautiously prepared a pot to take to a gathering of picky relatives. "How would they react?" I thought. "Would anyone like them?" Fortunately, they were a success, and I've made the dish for them several times since then.

MAIN DISHES

3 bouillon cubes

1 tsp. seasoning salt

1 tsp. garlic salt

½ tsp. black pepper

1 whole chicken, or equivalent amount of chicken

1 Tbsp. chopped garlic

2 (10.5-oz.) cans cream of mushroom soup

1 cup flour

2 (12-oz.) cans golden layer biscuits

additional seasonings

1. Fill a 6-quart stockpot approximately ⅔ full with water. Add bouillon cubes, seasoning salt, garlic salt, pepper, and garlic. Bring to a boil. Add chicken. Reduce heat to medium low and cook chicken until done.

2. Let chicken cool down in broth or remove chicken to cool on a plate. It is vitally important to retain the broth!

3. After chicken is cool enough to handle, remove chicken from the bones, shred or tear into bite-size pieces, and return to broth.

4. Add both cans of cream of mushroom soup to broth and put the pot on medium heat while you prepare dumplings.

5. To prepare the dumplings, use a large platter or two regular plates. Add flour to a plate. Place the biscuit dough on the flour. Working with one biscuit at a time, flatten each biscuit into a 4-inch round and slice each round into 16 pieces of dough. Make sure that each piece is coated in flour to prevent clumping. You will have a large amount of dumplings after preparing both cans

of biscuits. Give dumplings a toss in the flour to ensure that all of the dough is covered.

6. Bring the broth to a rapid boil before adding dumplings.

7. Once the broth is at a vigorous boil, add dumplings, including all of the flour, to the stockpot. Give the mixture a gentle stir to avoid sticking. The dumplings will swell and rise to the top of the pot. Don't panic! Give the mixture a few more stirs. At this point, you can sprinkle additional seasonings on top of the dumplings.

8. Lower the heat to medium and cover the pot. Let cook for 10 minutes.

9. Remove lid and stir again. The dumplings will have deflated by this point and stirring will combine the chicken and dumplings.

10. Lower the heat to medium low and cover the pot. Let cook for an additional 30 minutes until dumplings are thoroughly cooked.

11. Turn off heat and let dumplings rest for at least 30 minutes before eating.

BUTTERMILK *Chicken Fingers* WITH SPICY DIPPING SAUCE

Making homemade chicken fingers is the perfect way to stretch out a package of boneless chicken breasts. Three boneless chicken breasts can easily be turned into enough chicken fingers to feed 4–5 people.

3 boneless chicken breasts, sliced into thin strips

1 cup buttermilk

¼ cup hot sauce

½ tsp. black pepper

½ tsp. garlic salt

SAUCE

½ cup mayonnaise

1 tsp. Dijon mustard

1 Tbsp. hot sauce

¼ tsp. paprika

½ tsp. garlic powder

pinch of black pepper

1. Place all of the ingredients in a large zippered bag or covered bowl and refrigerate for at least 30 minutes.

2. While chicken is marinating, prepare sauce.

3. When ready to cook, add about one inch of canola or vegetable oil to a large skillet.

4. Fry chicken strips in batches over medium high heat until chicken is cooked through and golden brown, turning chicken through the cooking process, approximately 8 minutes.

5. Serve with dipping sauce.

6. For sauce, combine all ingredients together in a small bowl. Cover and refrigerate until ready to serve.

Honey Lime
CILANTRO
WINGS

Whenever I find chicken wings on sale, I like to grab a package or two to put in the freezer. On the weekends, my husband will often get a craving for wings and it's nice to be able to pull out a bag to thaw for dinner. The cilantro and lime really liven up the flavor and are two ingredients that I always try to have in my refrigerator.

½ cup chopped cilantro

1 tsp. lime zest

juice of 2 limes

¾ cup honey

1 Tbsp. sugar

1 tsp. soy sauce

½ tsp. garlic powder

1 tsp. salt

½ tsp. black pepper

1 Tbsp. minced garlic

4–5 lb. chicken wings

cilantro for garnishing, if desired

1. In a medium bowl, combine first ten ingredients. Cover and refrigerate for at least half an hour to allow flavors to blend together.

2. Meanwhile, place chicken wings in a large bowl. Sprinkle with salt and pepper, if desired.

3. Cover and refrigerate until sauce has had time to chill.

4. When ready to cook, grill the wings on low heat (between 300–325 degrees) for approximately 30 minutes before basting with the sauce.

5. Baste with sauce, turning the wings over until they're well coated.

6. Grill until done, approximately 45–50 minutes depending on your grill's heat level.

7. Sprinkle with fresh cilantro, if desired.

CITRUS CHICKEN WITH *Lemon Salt*

Lemon and chicken flavors work well together. I try to pick up a couple of lemons whenever I grocery shop because they're such a versatile fruit. There is no better scent in a kitchen than that of freshly grated lemon zest.

LEMON SALT

zest from 3 lemons

1 tsp. salt

1 Tbsp. chopped fresh parsley

CITRUS CHICKEN

3 lb. chicken (any combination of bone-in chicken pieces)

1 Tbsp. olive oil

¼ tsp. black pepper

3 lemons, quartered

1. Preheat oven to 350 degrees.
2. Prepare the lemon salt by combining all three ingredients. Set aside.
3. In a large baking dish greased with cooking spray, add chicken. Drizzle with olive oil and sprinkle with black pepper.
4. Place lemon wedges around the chicken.
5. Sprinkle lemon salt over the chicken.
6. Bake for one hour at 350 degrees.
7. Increase heat to 400 degrees and bake for an additional 10 minutes.

CHICKEN AND
Wild Rice
CASSEROLE

The beauty of this casserole is that you can use any chicken that is available to you—whole cut-up fryers or a variety of chicken parts. Chicken legs are on sale quite often and are perfect for this creamy, comforting casserole.

1 (6.2-oz.) pkg. long grain and wild rice

1 Tbsp. butter or margarine, cubed

3 cups chicken broth

3 lb. chicken (your choice of chicken pieces)

¼ tsp. salt

¼ tsp. black pepper

1 (10.5-oz.) can cream of mushroom soup

1 (1.1-oz.) packet onion soup mix

¼ tsp. paprika

1. Preheat oven to 350 degrees.

2. In a large 9 × 13 casserole dish, place the rice mixture and butter. Cover with chicken broth.

3. Place the chicken on top of the rice mixture and sprinkle with salt and pepper.

4. Spoon mushroom soup evenly over the chicken pieces.

5. Sprinkle onion soup mix evenly over the soup.

6. Sprinkle entire dish with paprika.

7. Cover with foil and bake for approximately 1 hour until chicken is done and rice has absorbed all of the broth.

LOW COUNTRY *Hash*

This is a recipe that floated around in my head for quite a while before becoming a reality. One of my family's favorite meals is a low country boil. As you may know, this can be an expensive meal to prepare. So I wanted to take the components of the boil and turn them into a more cost efficient dish. With this recipe, you will get all of the flavor of a low country boil for a fraction of the price.

1½ lb. red potatoes, cubed

1 Tbsp. salt

1 Tbsp. olive oil

14 oz. kielbasa sausage, sliced and quartered

½ tsp. seafood seasoning, divided

1 lb. raw, peeled shrimp

12 oz. frozen corn

1. In a large stockpot of water, bring potatoes and salt to a boil. Cook until tender and drain. Set aside.

2. In a large skillet over medium-high heat, add olive oil and sausage. Sprinkle with ¼ teaspoon of seafood seasoning. Cook until the sausage begins to brown around the edges.

3. Remove sausage with a slotted spoon and set aside, retaining the oil in the skillet.

4. To the remaining oil in the skillet, add shrimp along with ¼ teaspoon of seafood seasoning. Cook until shrimp are done, approximately 5 minutes.

5. Return sausage to the skillet. Add potatoes and corn.

6. Gently toss all ingredients together until corn is heated through.

7. Serve immediately.

Fish AND Grits

Growing up, a meal of fish and grits consisted of fried catfish served with a side of grits and fried hush puppies. In this recipe, I substituted tilapia, which I sautéed and served with a lemon-scented gravy.

4 tilapia filets

sprinkle of salt, pepper, and seafood seasoning

GRAVY

1 Tbsp. olive oil

½ bell pepper, finely diced

½ onion, finely diced

1 Tbsp. flour

2 cups chicken broth

½ cup water

juice from ½ lemon

⅛ tsp. seafood seasoning

½ tsp. garlic salt

pinch of salt

2 Tbsp. butter

2 cups prepared grits

1. Season the tilapia filets.

2. In a large skillet greased with cooking spray, cook fish in batches until done, flipping halfway through, approximately 6–8 minutes, depending upon thickness of fish. Remove from heat and set aside.

3. Add olive oil to the skillet and cook bell peppers and onions over medium heat until tender.

4. Add flour to make a roux and cook until golden brown.

5. Add broth, water, lemon juice, and seasonings. Cook until broth is thick and bubbly, approximately 8 minutes on medium heat.

6. Add butter and stir until melted.

7. To serve, place cooked fish on a bed of prepared grits. Cover with gravy.

8. Serve immediately.

SMOTHERED
Shrimp Bake

Whenever I cook or create a recipe, I always try to keep cost in mind, so there are some recipes that I don't prepare on a regular basis. This is a recipe that I save for special occasions, such as an anniversary or Christmas dinner. While I have included crabmeat in the list of ingredients, you may choose to omit it if your budget doesn't allow for the luxury.

1 Tbsp. olive oil

1 lb. shrimp, peeled and deveined

pinch of salt

SAUCE

½ green bell pepper, diced

½ medium onion, diced

1 tsp. olive oil

pinch of salt

2 (10.5-oz.) cans cream of celery soup

1 Tbsp. seafood seasoning

¼ tsp. black pepper

¼ tsp. garlic powder

1 Tbsp. lemon juice

4 dashes hot sauce

1 cup milk or chicken broth

8 oz. crabmeat

2–3 green onions, sliced

paprika

cooked rice or orzo

1. Preheat oven to 350 degrees.

2. In a large skillet, heat olive oil over medium-high heat. Add the shrimp and sprinkle with a pinch of salt. Cook for about 2 minutes.

3. Remove shrimp from the heat. Shrimp will not be done.

4. Spread out the shrimp in a casserole dish. Set aside.

5. Add diced bell pepper and onion to the same skillet that you used for the shrimp. Add teaspoon olive oil, sprinkle with salt, and cook until soft.

6. In a large bowl, add soup and bell pepper mixture.

7. Add dry seasonings and lemon juice.

8. Add hot sauce and milk or broth.

9. If using, add in the crabmeat.

10. Add green onions and stir to combine.

11. Pour this mixture over shrimp. Sprinkle with paprika.

12. Bake for 45 minutes.

13. Serve over rice or orzo.

SHRIMP SALAD
with *Potatoes*

This is the perfect recipe to make if you have a small amount of boiled shrimp that you would like to stretch out to feed several people.

1 cup mayonnaise

1 Tbsp. Dijon mustard

¼ tsp. black pepper

¼ tsp. garlic salt

3 green onions, thinly sliced

1 Tbsp. fresh dill

½ lb. boiled shrimp, cut into bite-size pieces

1 lb. boiled potatoes, cubed in bite-size pieces

1. In a large bowl, add all ingredients except shrimp and potatoes. Stir until well blended.

2. Gently stir in shrimp and potatoes until well coated.

3. Serve immediately or refrigerate until ready to serve.

FISH *Tacos*

I don't always order fish tacos at a Mexican restaurant, but I'm always satisfied whenever I do. There is just something about the combination of the sautéed fish, creamy dressing, and flour tortillas that make me want to eat one after the other. You can use your favorite fish in this dish.

4–6 white, flaky fish filets

sprinkling of Kosher salt, coarse black pepper, seafood seasoning

4–8 flour tortillas, depending on size

condiments of choice: salsa, pico de gallo, lettuce, cilantro, slaw mix, lime juice

1. Heat a nonstick skillet over medium-high heat. Spray with cooking spray.

2. Season both sides of filets with dry seasonings. Cook fish on each side, turning halfway through cooking process, until cooked through and the fish starts to flake, approximately 6–8 minutes. Be careful not to overcook.

3. Place cooked fish on flour tortillas, squeeze on a little fresh lime juice, and pile on your condiments.

Talapia WITH Lemon AND Capers

I love a white, flaky fish, so tilapia is my favorite fish to cook at home. It has such a neutral flavor that it can be used in many ways, with different flavor combinations. Wrapped in foil, this dish can be cooked in the oven or on the grill.

4–6 tilapia fillets

1 lemon

sprinkle of kosher salt and black pepper

1 Tbsp. capers

drizzle of olive oil

1. Prepare a large piece of aluminum foil with nonstick spray.

2. Zest the lemon and set aside.

3. Slice the lemon thinly and place on the foil in a single layer to serve as a bed for fish. The lemon provides flavor, as well as a base to prevent the fish from burning.

4. Season fish with salt and pepper and place on bed of lemon slices. Sprinkle with capers and lemon zest and drizzle with olive oil.

5. Form the foil into a packet and place on grill on the lowest heat setting. You may also cook the dish in a 350-degree oven.

6. Cook for 15–20 minutes, until the fish is flaky. Do not overcook!

7. Serve fish on a bed of rice or couscous.

MEXICAN *Beef*

My husband created this recipe. I came home from work one afternoon to find him standing at the stove attempting to breathe this dish into existence. We've tweaked the ingredients over the years and now it is absolutely perfect.

1½ lb. skirt steak

3 Tbsp. olive oil, divided

1 green bell pepper, julienned

1 large onion, julienned

2 Tbsp. garlic, chopped

½ tsp. seasoning salt

½ tsp. black pepper

½ tsp. garlic salt

12 oz. salsa

½ cup water

½ cup cilantro, chopped and divided

1. Prepare skirt steak by cutting it into thin slices. Set aside.

2. In a large skillet, heat 1 tablespoon of olive oil over medium-high heat and add bell peppers and onions.

3. After bell peppers and onions have been cooking for about 5 minutes, add garlic. Sauté until the vegetables have softened and caramelized, approximately 10 additional minutes. Remove from skillet. Set aside.

4. Season the steak with seasoning salt, pepper, and garlic salt. Add another tablespoon of olive oil to the skillet.

5. Divide the steak into batches so that it can brown and develop more flavor. Arrange just enough steak to cover the bottom of the skillet without letting the pieces overlap. Cook until the steak is brown on both sides, turning the steak over halfway through the cooking process, approximately 4 minutes per side over medium-high heat. Remove each batch of steak and set aside.

6. After all of the steak has been cooked, add it and the vegetables back into the skillet. Stir in the salsa, water, and half of the cilantro.

7. Cover the dish and let cook over medium-low heat for approximately 30 minutes until meat is thoroughly cooked and tender.

8. Sprinkle in the remaining cilantro.

9. Serve with rice.

SLOW COOKER *Pulled Pork*

Cooking pork in a slow cooker is less a recipe and more a process. This is my favorite way to eat pulled pork because the meat stays juicy and flavorful. To be honest, this recipe is the only reason that I own a slow cooker.

1 Boston butt or pork shoulder

seasoning of choice (I use seasoning salt, garlic salt, and black pepper)

½ cup water

barbecue sauce of choice

1. Spray a slow cooker with cooking spray.

2. Thoroughly coat the pork with the seasonings of your choice. If you choose to season your pork once you put it in the slow cooker, sprinkle some seasoning in the bottom of the slow cooker before adding the pork so the bottom of the meat will be seasoned on every side.

3. Add water to the slow cooker, cover, and turn it on low. Cooking times will vary based on the size of the meat, but I would dedicate 8–10 hours to it. It works well to cook it overnight, because it's always nice to wake up to a finished meal.

4. When the pork is done, drain all of the liquid from slow cooker. You will know the pork is done when it can easily be shredded with two forks.

5. Shred the pork and add desired amount of barbecue sauce. Stir in the sauce until evenly distributed.

6. Set the slow cooker to warm to let the sauce heat up and be absorbed into the meat.

7. Serve pulled pork on savory onions rolls with a splash of hot sauce or your favorite barbecue sauce.

Sausage & Potato BAKE

Because I always have kielbasa sausage in my freezer, this is one of those meals that I can throw together quickly. It does take a while to bake in the oven, but other than tossing it around occasionally so that it cooks evenly, it is a low-maintenance dish.

14 oz. kielbasa or smoked sausage, sliced

5–6 medium potatoes, peeled and cubed

1 large onion, cubed

seasonings to taste

olive oil to drizzle

1. Preheat oven to 350 degrees.

2. Combine sausage, potatoes, and onions in a lined and greased 9 × 13 baking dish.

3. Sprinkle with your favorite seasonings and drizzle with a little olive oil.

4. Bake until potatoes are done, about 1 hour, stirring every 10 minutes to keep potatoes from sticking.

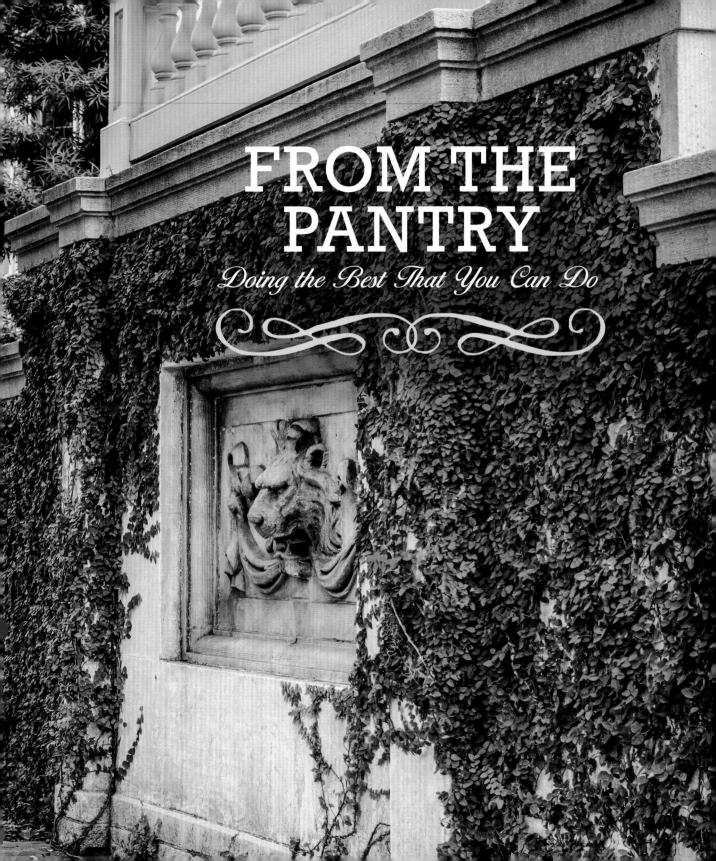

FROM THE PANTRY

Doing the Best That You Can Do

*P*antry—just hearing the word brings to mind a sense of comfort and security. As long as my pantry is stocked, I know that I can quickly prepare a meal for my family. What is my definition of pantry cooking? I consider pantry cooking being able to prepare a dish by simply using ingredients that I would normally have in my pantry and freezer, which also extends itself to the incorporation of leftovers.

My fondness for pantry cooking started when I was a stay-at-home mom to my two sons. Whenever it came time to plan the evening's meal, I would raid my cabinets and freezer to find meal ideas that did not involve me packing up my toddler and infant and driving us to the store for an ingredient or two. After I returned to work in a full-time capacity, I still relied on my pantry meals, because there were many times when I did not prepare ahead for the evening's meal.

This chapter holds a special place in my heart because it is meant to encourage you to use what ingredients you have on hand. You should never feel ashamed when you use convenience items, especially if those are the only items that you can afford. Yes, in a perfect world, we would all cook from scratch using organic ingredients. But the world is not perfect and finances are limited, and you should feel proud of yourself for doing the best that you can do. You fed your family, and no one can fault you for that.

CHICKEN CAESAR *Pasta Salad*

Because this recipe is the first of several pasta salad recipes in the cookbook, it should be known that I love pasta salad. I'm always drawn to pasta salads on menus, buffets, and potlucks and am continually brainstorming new pasta salad ideas. This recipe is a combination of two of my favorite dishes—Caesar salad and the beloved pasta salad.

8 oz. short pasta, prepared

4 oz. chicken breasts, cooked and diced

creamy Caesar dressing, divided

¼ tsp. black pepper

1 head romaine lettuce, cut into bite-size pieces

1 cup crushed croutons

1. In a large bowl, add cooked pasta, chicken, ¾ cup dressing, and black pepper. Stir until coated.

2. Add lettuce and crushed croutons. Stir gently until coated, adding more dressing as needed.

3. Serve immediately. If not eating immediately, wait until right before serving to add the lettuce and croutons.

FROM THE PANTRY

PEPPERONI PIZZA *Pasta Salad*

Born from the food festivals that my former coworkers and I used to throw, this salad was inspired by my friend Sarah, who brought a similar one to our first festival. I consumed a large amount of this salad at the time and re-created it here for everyone's enjoyment.

8 oz. pasta, prepared

2 oz. pepperoni, either mini pepperoni or quartered whole pepperoni

¼ green bell pepper, finely diced

2 green onions, thinly sliced

½ cup shredded Parmesan cheese

1 cup roasted red pepper vinaigrette, divided

1. In a large bowl, add pasta, pepperoni, vegetables, and cheese.

2. Add ¾ cup of vinaigrette. Chill until ready to serve. The pasta will absorb some of the dressing.

3. Right before serving, add remaining vinaigrette and blend well.

Ranch & Bacon
PASTA SALAD

This pasta salad sends me on the sentimental journey of a young woman who was being wooed by a young man. He invited her to his home for dinner and prepared a meal of grilled pork loin, corn, and a boxed pasta salad. She had never known pleasure until she locked lips with ranch and bacon pasta salad. She has eaten many boxes of the salad since then and has created her own recipe for the salad—and no longer needs the box. Just like her passion for this pasta salad, the young man is still hanging around too and is the father of her children.

8 oz. short pasta

1½ cups mayonnaise

1 Tbsp. ranch dressing mix

1 Tbsp. real bacon bits

3 green onions, chopped

1. Cook pasta in salted water (according to package directions), drain, and rinse.

2. In a bowl, mix together mayonnaise, dressing mix, bacon bits, and green onions until well blended.

3. Add drained pasta. Mix well. Eat now.

SOUTHWEST *Pasta Salad*

This pasta salad is perfect to serve alongside a meal of tacos or burritos. If you add some diced chicken, it can actually be a meal by itself.

12 oz. pasta

5 green onions, chopped

1 cup corn, drained and rinsed

½ cup black beans, drained and rinsed

1½ cups mayonnaise

1 Tbsp. ranch dressing mix

1 tsp. taco seasoning

½ tsp. garlic powder

½ cup fresh cilantro, chopped

1. Cook pasta in salted water, as directed. Drain and rinse.

2. Add green onions, corn, and black beans.

3. In a separate bowl, stir together mayonnaise and dried seasonings.

4. Stir cilantro into the mayonnaise mixture and pour mixture over the pasta. Enjoy!

LEFTOVER *Fried* *Chicken* SALAD

It's rare that we have fried chicken left over in our home. My husband and sons are all about the consumption of meat. However, occasionally I'll find a breast or thigh that's been forgotten (or hidden) in the refrigerator that I can use to make this leftover fried chicken salad. To stretch out the salad, throw in some chopped boiled eggs or cooked pasta.

2 fried chicken breasts and thighs, or combination of leftover fried chicken

1 cup mayonnaise

1 Tbsp. chopped chives

1 tsp. chopped dill

6 green onions, thinly sliced

½ tsp. garlic salt

½ tsp. garlic powder

¼ tsp. black pepper

1. Remove chicken from the bones and cut into bite-size pieces, retaining the fried chicken skin if possible.

2. Place chicken in a large bowl and add remaining ingredients.

3. Gently stir until combined.

FROM THE PANTRY

MEMA'S
Enchilada Casserole

Ah, the memories of this recipe . . . my Mema is 91 years old as I write this, and she no longer cooks. But when she was still in the kitchen, she could throw it down like a short-order cook. Whatever you wanted to eat, you would have it within a few minutes. If some of her grandchildren showed up, even unexpectedly, she would get busy making this enchilada casserole. We would eagerly eat it and love it.

1 lb. ground beef

1 onion, chopped

1 Tbsp. chopped garlic

½ tsp. seasoning salt

½ tsp. garlic salt

1 (10-oz.) can enchilada sauce

1 (10¾-oz.) can cream of chicken soup

1 (8-oz.) jar taco sauce

1 (12-oz.) bag nacho cheese tortilla chips, crushed

shredded cheese, optional

chopped cilantro, optional

1. Brown beef, adding onion, garlic, seasoning salt, and garlic salt. Drain well and return to skillet.

2. Add enchilada sauce, cream of chicken soup, and taco sauce. Stir well and bring to a simmer on medium-low heat.

3. Once the mixture has heated through, crush ⅓ of the chips and spread on the bottom of a greased casserole dish.

4. Add ½ of the beef mixture. Add another ⅓ of the crushed chips on top of the beef mixture. Add remaining beef mixture and top with remaining chips.

5. Bake at 350 degrees until heated through, about 30 minutes.

6. Add cheese, if desired, in the last few minutes of cooking.

POPPY SEED
Chicken Casserole

This is a dish that has been around for a while. I first had it at a family gathering where my aunt brought it. It was the topping with its combination of buttery crackers and garlic powder that sold me. I always thought that the recipe needed a little something to make it more substantial, so I've incorporated some cooked rice into the dish to stretch it out and make it a little more satisfying.

CASSEROLE TOPPING

1 sleeve buttery crackers, crushed

4 oz. or 1 stick margarine, melted

1 Tbsp. poppy seeds

¼ tsp. garlic powder

CASSEROLE FILLING

2 boneless chicken breasts, cooked and shredded

1 can cream of chicken soup

1 cup sour cream

1 cup cooked rice

¼ tsp. black pepper

¼ tsp. garlic powder

½ tsp. dried parsley flakes

1. Preheat oven to 350 degrees.
2. In a small bowl, prepare casserole topping by combining all ingredients. Set aside.
3. Place chicken in a bowl. Add soup and sour cream and blend well.
4. Stir in rice, black pepper, garlic powder, and parsley flakes.
5. Spread into a greased 9 × 13 baking dish.
6. Sprinkle cracker topping over chicken mixture.
7. Bake for 35–40 minutes until bubbly.

DEVILED
Tuna Casserole

One evening, I was desperate to find a meal to put on the table. I rummaged through my pantry and found a couple of cans of tuna and some elbow macaroni. As I drained the tuna and put it in a bowl to be seasoned, I had an idea. What if I seasoned the tuna as if I were making deviled crab cakes? The outcome was better than I had hoped. As my husband finished his first plate of the casserole, he asked, "Where did you get the crab?"

16 oz. elbow macaroni

2 (5-oz.) cans tuna, drained

2 (10½-oz.) cans cream of chicken soup

1 (15-oz.) can chicken broth

2 Tbsp. Dijon mustard

4–5 drops hot pepper sauce

1 tsp. seafood seasoning

¼ tsp. black pepper

¼ tsp. garlic salt

¼ tsp. seasoning salt

¼ tsp. paprika

TOPPING

¼ cup dried bread crumbs

¼ tsp. paprika

2 Tbsp. butter or margarine, softened

1. Preheat oven to 350 degrees.

2. Cook macaroni, drain, and set aside.

3. While macaroni is cooking, mix together tuna, soup, broth, mustard, hot sauce, and dry seasonings.

4. Add macaroni.

5. Put in a greased casserole dish. Sprinkle with bread crumbs. Sprinkle paprika onto bread crumbs and dot with margarine.

6. Bake for approximately 30 minutes until bubbly.

SAUCY
Baked Burritos

For some reason, I associate these burritos with Friday nights. Probably because they take some time and effort to make, so I make them on Friday nights as a welcome to the weekend meal. These burritos are delicious and well worth any effort that goes into them. I serve them with sides of black beans and yellow rice.

1 small onion, chopped

4–5 garlic cloves, chopped

1½–2 lb. ground beef

1 tsp. taco seasoning

1 tsp. garlic salt

½ cup chopped cilantro, divided

1 (10½-oz.) can tomato soup

1 (10½-oz.) can cream of mushroom soup

1 (10½-oz.) can enchilada sauce

6 large flour burrito-size tortillas

1. Preheat oven to 350 degrees.

2. In a large skillet over medium heat, sauté onion for five minutes. Add garlic, ground beef, taco seasoning, and garlic salt and cook until the beef is cooked through. When beef is done, drain and stir in a tablespoon of cilantro. Set aside.

3. In a small bowl, combine tomato soup, mushroom soup, and enchilada sauce. Add half of the remaining cilantro to the mixture.

4. Spray a 9 × 13 baking dish with cooking spray. Spread ½ cup of soup mixture on bottom of the baking dish to prevent the burritos from drying out. Add ¾ cup of soup mixture to the beef mixture and stir.

5. To prepare the burritos, you'll want to divide the beef mixture into six servings. You can just use your spoon to divide it in the skillet, estimating equal amounts of the mixture.

6. Fill first tortilla by placing beef mixture evenly down the middle of it.

7. Fold tortilla over on both sides of the mixture and place seam-side down in the prepared baking dish. Repeat process for remaining 5 tortillas.

8. Finish burritos by spreading remaining soup mixture evenly over burritos, making sure to cover all of the tortillas.

9. Bake until the soup mixture bubbles, 35–40 minutes.

10. Sprinkle remaining cilantro over the burritos when they come out of the oven.

QUICK
Curry Chicken

Another weeknight favorite, this chicken dish comes together fairly quickly. The smell of curry powder holds a special place in my husband's heart, because his parents traveled internationally before he was born, and his mother incorporated many exotic flavors into her cooking.

3 boneless chicken breasts (about 1½ lb.)

½ tsp. seasoning salt

½ tsp. garlic salt

¼ tsp. black pepper

1 onion, chopped

1 Tbsp. olive oil

1 (10½-oz.) can cream of chicken soup

1 cup milk

1 Tbsp. curry powder

1 tsp. dried parsley flakes

optional: chopped fresh cilantro

1. Cut chicken into one-inch cubes. Sprinkle with seasoning salt, garlic salt, and pepper. Set aside.

2. In a large skillet over medium heat, sauté onion in olive oil until soft and translucent. Do not brown. Remove onion from skillet and set aside. If skillet seems dry, add a little more oil.

3. Add chicken in a single layer (you may need to cook in batches) and cook until chicken is lightly brown on both sides. Add all chicken and onions back to the skillet.

4. In a small bowl, combine cream of chicken soup, milk, and curry powder. Pour over chicken and onion mixture. Add dried parsley flakes.

5. Bring mixture to a boil and then lower heat to medium low. Cover and cook for 15–20 minutes until chicken is completely done.

6. Add fresh cilantro if using. Serve over rice.

Skillet Sausage WITH PASTA

Grab a sausage out of your freezer and some pasta out of the pantry. You'll have this meal on the table in no time. This dish is simple and delicious.

1 onion, chopped

3 cloves garlic, chopped

1 tsp. olive oil

14-oz. kielbasa sausage, sliced

⅛ tsp. black pepper

½ tsp. garlic powder

1 Tbsp. dried parsley

2 cups chicken broth

8 oz. dried short pasta, prepared

PERFECT ADDITIONS

bell pepper, mushrooms, green onions, fresh herbs

1. In a large skillet, sauté onion and garlic in olive oil on medium heat for 3 minutes.
2. Add sliced kielbasa and sauté until heated through and the edges are caramelized, 10–12 minutes.
3. Add the seasonings and chicken broth. Cook until broth reduces down a little.
4. Stir in the prepared pasta and stir until well coated.
5. Serve immediately.

HOMEMADE
Beefy Noodle
SKILLET

This recipe is another homemade version of a boxed meal. One Saturday afternoon, my husband was craving the boxed version of this dish and was disappointed to find out that we didn't have one in our pantry. I took his craving as a personal challenge and informed him that I could create a homemade version better than the box. I could tell he doubted me, but a little later, when he sat on the couch with a bowl of my homemade beefy noodles, he admitted that homemade was better.

FROM THE PANTRY

1 lb. ground beef

2 cloves garlic

½ onion

¼ tsp. black pepper

½ tsp. garlic salt

1 (10½-oz.) can beef consommé

1 cup beef broth

8 oz. egg noodles

1 tsp. dried parsley

2 green onions, thinly sliced

1. In a large skillet over medium heat, add ground beef, garlic, onion, pepper, and garlic salt. Cook until beef has browned.

2. Drain and return meat mixture to skillet.

3. Add beef consommé and beef broth and bring to a rolling boil.

4. Add egg noodles and cook until done, approximately 10 minutes.

5. Remove from heat and sprinkle in the dried parsley and green onions.

6. Serve immediately.

KIM'S
Seasoning Mix

Since I tend to use the same seasoning blend over and over again, I thought it would be more convenient when cooking to combine the seasoning in one container. We reach for this mix every time we cook.

2 parts seasoning salt

2 parts garlic salt

1 part black pepper

1. Place in an empty spice container and shake to combine.

Cocktail Sauce

My husband is the king of cooking Low Country Boil. He also makes his own cocktail sauce. Over the years, I've inherited the task of making the sauce. I'm also sharing my knowledge with my older son, who is always up to sample and critique my work.

1 cup ketchup

1–2 Tbsp. horseradish,* depending on your tastes

1 tsp. hot sauce

juice from ½ of a lemon

* Jars of horseradish can be found in the dairy section of your grocery store.

1. These are the basic components of our cocktail sauce. Stir all ingredients together in a small bowl and refrigerate for at least 30 minutes to allow flavors to combine.

Tartar Sauce

> While I like cocktail sauce for boiled shrimp, I prefer tartar sauce for fried seafood. Here are two variations.

TRADITIONAL TARTAR SAUCE

This is the traditional tartar sauce that is served in most seafood restaurants in Georgia.

1 cup mayonnaise

1 tsp. yellow mustard

1 Tbsp. dill pickle relish (or a dill pickle diced into tiny pieces)

1 tsp. dill pickle juice

⅛ tsp. black pepper

¼ tsp. garlic powder

1. Combine all ingredients together in a small bowl. Cover and refrigerate until ready to use.

CAPER AND DILL TARTAR SAUCE

One of my favorite seafood restaurants in Charleston, South Carolina, inspired this tartar sauce. Upon a recent visit to the establishment, I was disappointed to learn that they no longer served it. I'm glad that I was able to experience the original and re-create it in my own kitchen.

1 cup mayonnaise

1 tsp. Dijon mustard

1 Tbsp. capers

1 tsp. chopped fresh dill

⅛ tsp. black pepper

¼ tsp. garlic powder

1. Combine all ingredients together in a small bowl. Cover and refrigerate until ready to use.

DESSERTS
Finishing on a (Sugar) High Note

Is there anything more enticing than a dessert table? Gathering desserts together in one area so that we're faced with an abundance of choices is a brilliant idea. Sometimes, some of us have been known to fix our dessert plates before our dinner plates just in case the dessert choices dwindle quickly.

Whenever we would have a gathering at Mema's house, we would place all of the dessert dishes on top of the large chest freezer in her kitchen. The freezer served as our dessert buffet. While there were always favorites—such as red velvet cake, pound cake, various pies, brownies, and cookies—I was always drawn to the surprise dessert that was kept in the refrigerator. Mema would always have a dessert in the refrigerator, and those cold, creamy desserts were always my favorite. Sometimes, it would be a blueberry torte or a cake with creamy

frosting and sliced strawberries. It didn't matter which dessert I found there, I knew it would be my favorite.

As you can see here in this selection of recipes, I don't make complicated desserts. Simple desserts are always crowd-pleasers. While I do make a lot of cakes from scratch (especially pound cakes) I have included several recipes here that use boxed cake mixes. Why? Because that's reality. Many people of all ages, from all areas of this country, like to use cakes mixes sometimes. It's nothing to be ashamed of, nor should anyone be made to feel ashamed for using them. If you prefer to substitute the cake in these recipes for scratch cakes, you're more than welcome to do so. For those of you who are not scratch bakers, I hope that you will be able to enjoy these recipes and feel a sense of accomplishment when you have prepared them.

RASPBERRY *White Chocolate Cheesecake* COOKIES

Some recipes I create with certain people in mind. My friend Judith loves raspberry white chocolate chip cookies. She will sometimes grab a few for us when she visits the local chain sandwich restaurant. I wanted to make a homemade version of the cookie in her honor.

1 cup butter, softened

1 cup sugar

1 (3.5-oz.) pkg. cheesecake flavored instant pudding mix

2 eggs

1 tsp. vanilla

2¼ cups flour

1 tsp. baking soda

1 (12-oz.) pkg. white chocolate chips

1 cup raspberry preserves

1. In a large mixing bowl, blend together butter, sugar, and pudding mix until smooth.

2. Add eggs and vanilla. Mix until smooth.

3. Add in flour and baking soda and mix until thoroughly blended. Stir in white chocolate chips and refrigerate dough for 30 minutes before using.

4. When ready to bake, preheat oven to 350 degrees. Line a baking sheet with parchment paper.

5. Form the dough into twenty-four 1-inch balls and flatten slightly on baking sheet, leaving some dough for the top.

6. Add ¼ teaspoon of raspberry preserves to each cookie dough ball.

7. Take another ½ teaspoon of cooking dough and flatten into a disk about the size of a quarter.

8. Place on top of the raspberry filling.

9. Bake for 10–12 minutes.

Yields 24 cookies

Apple Pie
THUMBPRINT
COOKIES

My favorite combination of flavors is apple and cinnamon. I'll choose an apple cinnamon dessert over any other. Just biting into that gooey center of apple filling makes me so happy.

DESSERTS

COOKIES

1 cup butter, softened

⅔ cup sugar

1 tsp. vanilla

2 cups flour

1 tsp. apple pie spice

½ cup apple jam or jelly

GLAZE

1 cup powdered sugar

½ tsp. vanilla

2–3 tsp. water or milk

1. In a large bowl, cream butter, sugar, and vanilla until smooth.

2. Add flour and apple pie spice. Mix until well incorporated. The mixture will be thick and crumbly.

3. Use your hands to press the mixture into a flat disk, cover with plastic wrap, and refrigerate until chilled, about an hour.

4. When ready to bake, preheat oven to 350 degrees. Form dough into 1-inch balls and place on parchment paper–lined cookie sheet.

5. Using the back of a measuring spoon or your thumb, press an indention into the dough. Fill with apple jam.

6. Bake for approximately 15 minutes or until lightly brown. Cool completely.

7. In a small bowl, mix all ingredients for glaze and drizzle over cooled cookies.

Yields 24 cookies

Peach Cobbler COOKIES

Since I'm from the South, I have to like peach cobbler. Or I have to say I like peach cobbler. I like the peaches but not so much the texture of the cobbler. So I was inspired to deconstruct peach cobbler and re-create it as a cookie—same flavor with a better texture.

COOKIES

1 cup butter, softened

⅔ cup sugar

1 tsp. vanilla

2 cups flour

½ tsp. cinnamon

PEACH FILLING

2 peaches, peeled and finely diced

3 Tbsp. peach or apricot preserves

⅛ tsp. cinnamon

1 Tbsp. sugar

1. In a large bowl, cream butter, sugar, and vanilla until smooth.

2. Add flour and cinnamon. Mix until well incorporated. The mixture will be thick and crumbly.

3. Use your hands to press mixture into a flat disk, cover with plastic wrap, and refrigerate until chilled, about an hour.

4. Prepare peach filling by combining all ingredients in a small bowl. Set aside.

5. When ready to bake, preheat oven to 350 degrees. Form dough into 1-inch balls and place on parchment paper–lined cookie sheet.

6. Using the back of a measuring spoon or your thumb, press an indention into dough. Fill with peach filling.

7. Bake for approximately 15 minutes or until lightly brown. Cool completely.

Yields 24 cookies

DESSERTS

Italian Cream COOKIES

The classic ingredients of an Italian cream cake—coconut, pecans, and cream cheese frosting—turned into a cookie. The flavors are rich and sweet, but you'll feel less guilty eating a cookie than you would a slice of cake.

COOKIES

½ cup butter, softened

1 cup sugar

1 egg

1 tsp. vanilla

2½ cups flour

½ tsp. baking soda

½ tsp. salt

½ cup buttermilk

½ cup shredded sweetened coconut

½ cup finely chopped pecans

FROSTING

1 (8-oz.) pkg. cream cheese, softened

½ stick or 4 oz. butter, softened

1 tsp. vanilla

2 cups powdered sugar

1 cup shredded sweetened coconut

1 cup finely chopped pecans

1. Preheat oven to 375 degrees.

2. In a large bowl, mix butter and sugar until creamy. Mix in egg and vanilla.

3. In a small bowl, combine flour, baking soda, and salt. Add buttermilk and flour to the butter mixture, alternating between the two. Stir in coconut and pecans.

4. Drop by rounded tablespoonfuls onto parchment-lined baking sheets.

5. Bake 10–12 minutes or until lightly browned around the edges.

6. Cool completely before frosting.

7. For frosting, mix together cream cheese, butter, vanilla, and powdered sugar in a medium-sized bowl.

8. Stir in coconut.

9. Frost each cookie and sprinkle with chopped pecans.

10. Any leftover frosting can be frozen for a later use, like a secret midnight snack.

Yields 24 cookies

Toffee & Brown Sugar
RICE CEREAL TREATS

It's really hard to improve on the original rice cereal treat. I have enjoyed many pans of them over the years. But sometimes I get ideas that nag me until I give in to the temptation. A little voice inside of me kept saying, "Add some brown sugar and toffee chips to the treats. What's the worst that can happen?" Nothing bad happened. In fact, the results were extremely good.

¼ cup butter (plus 1 Tbsp. for greasing the pan)

1 (10-oz.) pkg. miniature marshmallows

½ cup brown sugar

5 cups puffed rice cereal

¾ cup toffee chips, divided

1. Prepare a 9 × 13 baking dish by coating the bottom and sides with 1 Tbsp. of butter.

2. In a large stockpot, melt ¼ cup butter and marshmallows, gradually adding the brown sugar until fully blended. Remove from heat.

3. Add the cereal and ½ cup toffee bits. Gently press into the prepared pan.

4. Sprinkle the remaining toffee bits on top, if desired.

5. Let the mixture cool completely and cut into squares.

DESSERTS

DEBORAH'S
Pecan Pie

One fall, I set out to master the art of making pecan pies. I tried recipe after recipe—pecan pie with caramel, pecan pie with chocolate—and all were delicious and successful. When my friend Deborah learned of my pecan pie quest, she insisted that I try her recipe. This recipe calls for margarine, which is cheaper than butter. However, butter may be substituted if you prefer. This recipe makes two basic but delicious pecan pies and is the perfect recipe to launch your own pecan pie quest.

3 eggs

½ cup or 1 stick of margarine, melted

1 cup sugar

¾ cup light corn syrup

¼ tsp. salt

1 tsp. vanilla

1½ cups pecans, chopped

2 standard pie shells

1. In a large mixing bowl, beat eggs until frothy. Add margarine, sugar, corn syrup, salt, and vanilla. Stir until well blended.

2. Add pecans. Stir until pecans are evenly distributed.

3. Pour the filling into the two pie shells, dividing as evenly as possible. You could also use the filling to bake one deep-dish pie, but your cooking time will increase.

4. Bake at 375 degrees for 40 minutes, watching closely to make sure the crusts are not getting too brown. If they are, add a foil collar around the crusts.

5. When the pie is done, the pecans should be glossy and the filling should be slightly firm to the touch. The filling will set up completely as the pie cools.

6. Allow pies to cool completely before slicing. (I actually prefer to refrigerate my pecan pies overnight before cutting.)

DESSERTS

Strawberry Cream PIE

Something about the combination of strawberries with cream cheese and powdered sugar is so decadent. A fresh strawberry pie is definitely going to draw some admirers. Make this for your next gathering.

1 (9-in.) prepared deep-dish pie crust, baked (or a graham cracker crust)

1 (8-oz.) pkg. cream cheese, softened

½ cup powdered sugar

1 tsp. vanilla

1 (8-oz.) container whipped topping, thawed and divided

1 (16-oz.) container fresh strawberries

1. If you're using a regular pie crust, bake it until completely done. Set aside.

2. In a large bowl, beat cream cheese until smooth. Add the powdered sugar and vanilla. Blend well.

3. Add half of the whipped topping to the cream cheese mixture and blend until smooth.

4. Dice about ¼ of the strawberries. It should equal about ¾ cup of strawberries.

5. Fold diced strawberries into the cream cheese mixture. Spread the mixture into prepared crust.

6. Spread the remaining whipped topping on top of the cream cheese mixture.

7. Slice the remaining strawberries and place on top of the whipped topping.

8. Refrigerate until completely chilled.

DESSERTS

Banana Pudding
CAKE

I don't think I've ever been to a gathering where there wasn't a dish of banana pudding. I'm always going to get a big scoop on my plate because I love it so. But here's a little secret about banana pudding that you might not know. The bananas don't hold up well over time. They become brown and soggy. I've found that you have about 24 hours to make and consume the pudding before all is lost. That's why I created the banana pudding cake where the banana flavor is coming from banana pudding mix instead of actual bananas. This cake has all of the flavor of a banana pudding but with a slightly extended life.

CAKE

1 (16.5-oz.) box butter flavored cake mix

4 eggs

1 cup sour cream

⅓ cup butter, softened

¼ cup water

¼ cup sugar

1 tsp. vanilla

FROSTING

1 (3.9-oz.) box banana cream instant pudding mix

¼ cup powdered sugar

1 cup milk

1 (8-oz.) container whipped topping, thawed

1 cup crushed vanilla wafer crumbs

1. Preheat oven to 350 degrees.
2. Grease a 9 × 13 baking pan and set aside.
3. In a large bowl, mix all of the ingredients together until well blended. Spread evenly in the prepared baking pan and bake for 25–30 minutes until done.
4. Let cool completely.
5. For frosting, add pudding and powdered sugar in a large mixing bowl.
6. Add milk. Beat with a mixer until smooth.
7. Fold in whipped topping until fully incorporated into pudding mixture. Spread on the cooled cake.
8. Sprinkle with crushed vanilla wafer crumbs.
9. Refrigerate until ready to serve.

DESSERTS

BARBARA'S
Red Velvet CAKE

The dessert that I associate most with the Christmas holidays is my aunt's red velvet cake. She makes it with four layers of cake, covered with rich cream cheese and pecan frosting. It is so rich that it's almost impossible to eat a whole piece at one time. I prefer to prepare the cake as a sheet cake instead of a layer cake to cut down on the richness of the frosting. Pecans are optional, because they can often be expensive.

CAKE

1⅔ cups sugar

1½ cups vegetable oil

2 eggs

1 tsp. vanilla

1 tsp. vinegar

1 (1-oz.) bottle red food coloring

2½ cups self-rising flour

1 tsp. baking soda

1 tsp. baking cocoa

1 cup buttermilk

TRADITIONAL CREAM CHEESE PECAN ICING

4 oz. or 1 stick margarine, softened

1 (8-oz.) pkg. cream cheese, softened

1 tsp. vanilla

1 (32-oz.) pkg. powdered sugar

1 Tbsp. milk

2 cups chopped pecans (optional)

1. Preheat oven to 350 degrees.

2. Traditionally, this recipe is prepared in four 9-inch layer cakes, but you may also make this as a sheet cake, according to your preference. Prepare four 9-inch baking pans with baking spray or with shortening and flour.

3. In a large mixing bowl, combine sugar, vegetable oil, eggs, vanilla, and vinegar. Blend until smooth. Slowly and carefully, add red food coloring.

4. In a small bowl, combine the flour, baking soda, and cocoa.

5. Alternately, add flour mixture and buttermilk to sugar mixture, beginning and ending with flour.

6. Place batter into prepared pans and bake for 20–25 minutes.

7. After cakes are done, place onto cooling racks. Let cakes cool completely before frosting.

8. For frosting, mix margarine and cream cheese until smooth in a large mixing bowl. Add vanilla. Beat until smooth.

9. Slowly add in small amounts of powdered sugar until blended. When mixture starts to thicken, add milk. If frosting is thicker than you prefer, add a little more milk, 1 teaspoon at a time.

10. When frosting is thoroughly blended, stir in pecans, or press pecans to the sides of the cake after it has been frosted.

CLASSIC
Vanilla Cupcakes

People get really fancy with cupcakes. The flavor varieties and combinations are endless. While I can appreciate the effort and creativity that goes into baking these fancy cupcakes, I prefer to keep it simple. My favorite cupcake is a yellow cake with vanilla frosting. There's no almond flavoring to this girl. I'm a purist. Vanilla is best. This is the recipe that my cousins use whenever they make cakes, which is quite often.

CAKE

1 (16.5-oz.) box yellow cake mix

4 eggs

1 cup sour cream

⅓ cup butter, softened

¼ cup milk

¼ cup sugar

1 tsp. vanilla

VANILLA FROSTING

1 cup butter, softened

1 cup shortening

2 tsp. vanilla

1 pinch salt

1 (32-oz.) pkg. powdered sugar

2–3 Tbsp. milk

1. Preheat oven to 350 degrees.

2. Blend all cake ingredients together in a large mixing bowl until smooth.

3. Place cupcake liners in muffin tins and fill ⅔ full with cake batter.

4. Bake 15–20 minutes, until toothpick comes out clean when testing.

5. For vanilla frosting, cream butter and shortening in a large mixing bowl until smooth. Add vanilla and salt. Mix until incorporated into butter mixture.

6. Slowly add powdered sugar in small increments until thoroughly mixed. Add milk by teaspoons as the mixture starts to thicken. The total amount of milk will depend upon how thick you like your frosting.

7. Put finished frosting in a piping bag fitted with your favorite tip and generously cover your cupcakes.

Yields 24 cupcakes

DESSERTS

APPLE PIE
Cheesecake Bites

Apple pie and cheesecake work well together. Decorate the top with a Red Delicious apple to add more color.

1 (8-oz.) pkg. cream cheese, softened

1 cup brown sugar

1 egg

1 tsp. vanilla

½ tsp. cinnamon

1 large apple, any variety, finely diced

2 (15-count) pkgs. mini fillo shells

1. Preheat oven to 350 degrees.
2. In a large bowl, combine cream cheese, brown sugar, egg, vanilla, and cinnamon. Blend until smooth.
3. Gently fold in diced apples.
4. Place the fillo shells on a baking sheet lined with foil or parchment paper.
5. Carefully spoon cream cheese mixture into shells.
6. Top with additional apple pieces, if desired.
7. Bake for approximately 15 minutes.
8. Allow to cool before serving.

DESSERTS

Fifth Avenue BARS

Before the world knew about the phenomenon known as gooey butter cakes, my family was serving Fifth Avenue Bars at our showers and parties. Thinner than the gooey butter cake, these bars are always a hit at any event.

CRUST

1 (16½-oz.) yellow or butter-flavored cake mix

½ cup butter, melted

1 egg

FILLING

1 (8-oz.) package cream cheese, softened

2 eggs

1 tsp. vanilla

1 (16-oz.) box powdered sugar

1. In a large bowl, prepare the crust by combining all crust ingredients. Blend with a mixer. The mixture will be thick.

2. Pour the mixture into a greased and foil-lined 15 × 10 pan. Press the mixture evenly on the bottom of the pan.

3. Using the same bowl, prepare the filling by blending the cream cheese, eggs, and vanilla together until smooth.

4. Add powdered sugar a little at a time until all of it is fully blended. Spread filling over the crust.

5. Bake at 350 degrees for approximately 30 minutes until golden brown.

6. Cool completely, preferably overnight.

7. Cut into squares.

Blueberry Torte CAKE

This is one of the desserts that Mema would have chilling in her refrigerator at family gatherings. While you could use a canned pie filling, this recipe is the perfect way to use up the abundance of summer blueberries that are often forced upon us.

CAKE

1 (16½-oz.) box yellow cake mix

4 eggs

1 cup sour cream

⅓ cup butter, softened

¼ cup milk

¼ cup sugar

1 tsp. vanilla

BLUEBERRY FILLING

2 pt. blueberries, divided

½ cup sugar

1 lemon, zested and juiced

¼ cup water

CREAM CHEESE FILLING

1 (8-oz.) pkg. cream cheese, softened

1 cup powdered sugar

1 tsp. vanilla

1 (8-oz.) container frozen whipped topping, thawed

1. Preheat oven to 350 degrees.

2. Blend all cake ingredients together in a large mixing bowl until smooth. Pour into a prepared 9 × 13 baking pan and bake for approximately 25 minutes or until toothpick tested in the middle of cake comes out clean.

3. While cake is baking, prepare blueberry filling.

4. Cool cake completely before adding filling.

5. For blueberry filling, set aside one cup of blueberries.

6. In a medium saucepan, add remaining blueberries, sugar, lemon zest and juice, and water.

7. Cook on medium-low heat for 20 minutes until slightly thickened. Add remaining blueberries.

8. Turn off heat and let cool completely before adding to cake.

9. For cream cheese filling, mix cream cheese, powdered sugar, and vanilla in a medium bowl, until thoroughly blended. Fold in whipped topping.

10. When ready to assemble cake, spread cream cheese filling evenly over cooled cake.

11. Spoon blueberry filling evenly over cream cheese layer.

12. Cover the dish with plastic wrap or aluminum foil and keep refrigerated.

Milk & Cookies
FROZEN DESSERT

The first time I ate this dessert, I was absolutely floored when I found out the ingredients were: milk, chocolate chip cookies, and whipped topping. When I made this at home and gave my son a piece, he told me it was the best dessert that I've ever made. That's high praise coming from a child who will only eat brownies.

1 cup milk

1 (18.2-oz.) family size pkg. of store-bought crunchy chocolate chip cookies

1 (12-oz.) container frozen whipped topping, thawed

1. Pour milk into a small bowl.

2. Dip one chocolate chip cookie at a time in the milk and place in a single layer in a casserole or serving dish.

3. Spoon ⅓ of the whipped topping over the cookies. Repeat this process two more times, ending with the whipped topping.

4. Cover the dish with plastic wrap or foil and place in the freezer. Allow to freeze completely.

5. Bring the dish out about 10 minutes before serving to make it easier to serve.

DESSERTS

Brownie TRIFLE

If you want to make a dessert that draws attention at a gathering, make a trifle. It doesn't matter what kind of trifle you make, as long as it's a layered dessert in a trifle dish. People are drawn to the trifle dish. They must have it, whatever it is. To make the people even crazier, make it a brownie trifle layered with chocolate mousse and toffee bits.

1 (9 × 13) pan of prepared brownies

1 (24-oz.) carton heavy whipping cream

1 (3.9-oz.) pkg. instant chocolate pudding mix

1 (12-oz.) container frozen whipped topping, thawed and divided

1 cup chocolate-covered toffee bars, finely chopped

1. Cut prepared brownies into bite-size pieces. Add ⅓ of the brownie pieces into the bottom of a trifle bowl.

2. In a large mixing bowl, add heavy whipping cream and pudding mix. Whip together until light and fluffy.

3. Spread ⅓ of mixture over brownies in bowl.

4. Add ⅓ of whipped topping over the chocolate pudding layer.

5. Add ⅓ of chopped candy bars on whipped topping layer.

6. Repeat the process two more times.

7. Cover and refrigerate until serving.

KEY LIME PIE
Éclair

Zesting citrus is one of my favorite things to do in the kitchen. I absolutely love the smell of lime and lemon zest. This is another chilled dessert that is easy to assemble and absolutely delicious!

1 (8-oz.) pkg. cream cheese, softened

1 (14-oz.) can sweetened condensed milk

⅓ cup key lime juice

2 (8-oz.) containers frozen whipped topping, thawed

graham crackers

1 tsp. lime zest

1. In a large mixing bowl, combine cream cheese, condensed milk, and lime juice.

2. Gently fold in one container of whipped topping.

3. In a serving dish, place one layer of graham crackers across the bottom of the dish.

4. Add ½ of cream cheese mixture.

5. Repeat the process with another layer of crackers, followed by the rest of the cream cheese mixture.

6. Finish with a layer of whipped topping and sprinkle with lime zest.

7. Cover and refrigerate until serving. (I recommend refrigerating overnight to soften the crackers.)

DESSERTS

COOKING MEASUREMENT EQUIVALENTS

Cups	Tablespoons	Fluid Ounces
⅛ cup	2 Tbsp.	1 fl. oz.
¼ cup	4 Tbsp.	2 fl. oz.
⅓ cup	5 Tbsp. + 1 tsp.	
½ cup	8 Tbsp.	4 fl. oz.
⅔ cup	10 Tbsp. + 2 tsp.	
¾ cup	12 Tbsp.	6 fl. oz.
1 cup	16 Tbsp.	8 fl. oz.

Cups	Fluid Ounces	Pints/Quarts/Gallons
1 cup	8 fl. oz.	½ pint
2 cups	16 fl. oz.	1 pint = ½ quart
3 cups	24 fl. oz.	1½ pints
4 cups	32 fl. oz.	2 pints = 1 quart
8 cups	64 fl. oz.	2 quarts = ½ gallon
16 cups	128 fl. oz.	4 quarts = 1 gallon

Other Helpful Equivalents

1 Tbsp.	3 tsp.
8 oz.	½ lb.
16 oz.	1 lb.

METRIC MEASUREMENT EQUIVALENTS

Approximate Weight Equivalents

Ounces	Pounds	Grams
4 oz.	¼ lb.	113 g
5 oz.		142 g
6 oz.		170 g
8 oz.	½ lb.	227 g
9 oz.		255 g
12 oz.	¾ lb.	340 g
16 oz.	1 lb.	454 g

Approximate Volume Equivalents

Cups	US Fluid Ounces	Milliliters
⅛ cup	1 fl. oz.	30 ml
¼ cup	2 fl. oz.	59 ml
½ cup	4 fl. oz.	118 ml
¾ cup	6 fl. oz.	177 ml
1 cup	8 fl. oz.	237 ml

Other Helpful Equivalents

½ tsp.	2½ ml
1 tsp.	5 ml
1 Tbsp.	15 ml

NOTES

NOTES

NOTES

NOTES

INDEX

INDEX

ABOUT THE AUTHOR

With a bachelor's degree in English, Kimberly began writing the food blog *A Well-Seasoned Life* in 2010. From 2011 to 2012, she wrote a weekly food blog for her local newspaper, *Effingham Now*, a branch of the Savannah News Press (http://savannahnow.com/authors/kim-mccallie). She has reviewed cookbooks for numerous publishers while privately developing her own original recipes and content for future publications.

Throughout the years, Kimberly has worked outside of the home and as a stay-at-home mom, both positions affording her the opportunity to create frugal yet delicious recipes. She lives near Savannah, Georgia, with her husband and their two sons, ages eleven and thirteen.

SCAN to visit

WWW.WELLSEASONEDLIFE.NET